Difficulties in the Analytic Encounter

CLASSICAL PSYCHOANALYSIS AND ITS APPLICATIONS

A Series of Books
Edited by Robert Langs, M.D.

Difficulties in the Analytic Encounter

John Klauber

M.A., B.M., B. Ch. (Oxon.), F.R.C. Psych., F.B. Ps. S.

Jason Aronson

New York • *London*

Copyright 1981 by Jason Aronson, Inc.

ISBN: 0-87668-430-4

Library of Congress Catalog Number 80-69670

10 9 8 7 6 5 4 3 2 1

Manufactured in the United States of America.

To Ruth
with love and thanks

Contents

Part III
DIFFICULTIES IN THE ANALYST

Acknowledgments

I greatly appreciate the help I received from Mrs. Gweneth Enfield, who typed the manuscript and whose patience is unmatched.

I am also grateful for permission to reprint articles from the *International Journal of Psycho-Analysis,* the *International Review of Psycho-Analysis,* and the *British Journal of Medical Psychology.* Following is a list of the original titles and sources of the chapters in this volume.

Chapter 1: On the significance of reporting dreams in psychoanalysis. *International Journal of Psycho-Analysis* 48 (1967).

Chapter 2: On the relationship of transference and interpretation in psychoanalytic therapy. *International Journal of Psycho-Analysis* 53 (1972).

Chapter 3: Some little-described elements of the psychoanalytical relationship and their therapeutic implications. *International Review of Psycho-Analysis* 3 (1976).

Chapter 4: Analyses that cannot be terminated. *International Journal of Psycho-Analysis* 58 (1977).

Chapter 5: Die Struktur der Psychoanalytischen Sitzung als Leitlinie für die Deutungarbeit. *Psyche* 20 (1966).

Chapter 6: An attempt to differentiate a typical form of transference in neurotic depression. *Internaional Journal of Psycho-Analysis* 47 (1966).

INTRODUCTION

Arriving at Solutions

What one writes is primarily for oneself. The more I thought about the request to compile a book of some of my papers, the more it seemed to me that they represented my struggles to find solutions to difficulties in the analytic encounter. It also appeared to me that whenever I had succeeded in formulating my views, they had struck a responsive chord in enough people whose opinion I respected to give me the confidence to publish them. I have also thought that to acknowledge the personal struggle and describe some aspects of it may be the most important contribution that I can make to psychoanalysis. That is the aim of this introduction.

One becomes a psychoanalyst because of the relationship of psychoanalysis to truth. The revelation of new truth about the human psyche in Freud (for me originally in Jung) was overwhelming. Of course ambivalence and scepticism were also stirred. Could one really believe, for instance, that if one dreamt that one had been to a place before, one was dreaming of one's mother's genitals because there was no other place of which one could assert this with such certainty? But by and large I felt that psychoanalytic interpretation must inevitably be therapeutic. "Truth is the food of minds." How could truth not heal?

This is still my attitude to psychoanalysis. I believe that truth is the great corrective by which, with the analyst's help, patients heal themselves. It is not the only thing to be valued in life. Man lives by fantasy as well as by truth, and this must be true of scientists too, including psychoanalysts. However, if a scientist's faith in the power of science to solve problems or his commitment to a theory goes beyond what is rationally justified, it is disturbing. Psychoanalysis has no public standards of validation comparable to those developed over centuries in the natural sciences. Its methods of investigation are private, clinical, and even personal. There is a danger, which Freud illustrated, that its theories, especially its metatheories, may shade off into metaphysics. This leaves the uncomfortable feeling that psychoanalysts may sometimes confuse a personal philosophy they have incorporated with scientific explanation.

I will therefore try to describe the development of my thought, not, I hope, entirely for egotistical reasons, but because I know that my feelings are not unique. I remember a much respected older analyst telling me how intimidating the atmosphere was in the early days of psychoanalysis in her native country. There was a time in my memory when an analyst putting forward a new insight would only too frequently feel it necessary to end with a statement that the new view was not really a departure from Freud's teaching. I think the atmosphere in many psychoanalytic societies has changed, but I still doubt if I need to multiply examples of a tendency to dogmatism. There are reasons for this attitude which go beyond any reluctance to give sufficient acknowledgment to uncertainties. Psychoanalysis is a highly exacting discipline. It is constantly threatened with dilution, and students require a consistent framework of clinical theory if their therapy is not to become arbitrary. Nonetheless, such demands for discipline as a guarantee of professional identity have their perils. In this introduction I describe the latent development of my thought (which I understood only very imperfectly at the time). I hope that it will contribute to a freer recognition of some of the difficulties in the path of becoming a psychoanalyst.

When I entered psychoanalytic training in 1948 at the age of thirty-one, I had read almost all Freud's books and about half his collected papers. The first thing that struck me was how different the experience of analysis was from my expectations of it from the literature—a contrast that Freud himself emphasized when he stated that conviction about the truth of analysis was more easily acquired by entering analysis than by reading accounts of it. I learned first that lying on the couch and associating freely is very frightening. I learned that even a comparatively stable person can be carried into action in a disconcerting way by emotions he does not understand. I learned that a hint of the analyst's displeasure, even though one knew that the analyst had misunderstood one, could bring an advance to an abrupt end. I learned the amazing therapeutic power of simple, well-directed interpretation. I learned, and have never forgotten, how much a patient can improve with scarcely any interpretation. And I learned how a patient could be prevented from expressing important attitudes or prejudices by the disinclination of the analyst to accept them. In other words, I learned some of the realities of the transference (and perhaps also of the countertransference) that had defied description, as Freud had indicated, but I have never been convinced that a more thoroughgoing attempt should not be made.

These experiences are no doubt individual. No technique can be expected to be proof against all vicissitudes. But they had the effect of alerting me to the importance of unresolved difficulties which may accompany other analyses, including training analyses. I try to base my own technique on one cardinal assumption. This is that psychoanalysis is a long process in which what happens after the patient has left the psychoanalyst's consulting room for the last time is more important than what happens during the analysis. By this I mean that the process which is started, with the patient's independence as its aim, is the prime consideration of therapy. That psychoanalysis aims at development and not cure is generally recognized, and yet I think that our technique often does not take sufficient account of it. One is reluctant to terminate before something like a cure is achieved; it means that something is still preventing the patient's development, and one wishes to analyze the inhibition rather than trust to the future. But analysts frequently overrate the significance of cures achieved during the actual process of analysis and underrate the frequency with which the patient does not accept "termination," but after an interval moves to a second analyst.

The unresolved problems that I wish to discuss are of an intellectual and technical kind. I only realized gradually that their roots lay in problems of the analysis of the transference, and especially of the special type of transference that a psychoanalyst forms with his own analyst. A psychoanalyst does not bring only his personal transference. Behind this he brings a transference of admiration and suspicion toward the great leader whose representative his analyst is. The difficulty is that his ability to do his professional work demands that he should identify with this leader despite his ambivalence and before he has completed the years of work necessary to come to a proper judgment. What prompted me to write these papers, I now see, was my wish to clarify my views on psychoanalysis and resolve these supercharged elements of the transference—and, if I could reach my own truth, to have it recognized by others.

The first problem that besets a newly qualified psychoanalyst is of course to understand his patients. This is especially hard for a psychoanalyst with little experience of psychotherapy, as is the case with many nonmedical analysts, and also happened to be the case with me. One requirement was obviously to acquire more knowledge of the literature than a part-time training on three evenings a week could give. But the newly qualified analyst is still confronted with the immense difficulty of integrating theory and practice. The ability to formulate in metapsychological terms comes only slowly. To some analysts it comes very slowly indeed. Yet it is essential. Without a mastery of Freud's language his thought cannot be fully understood or communicated, and a confusion of tongues arises. The reasons for this disjunction (which clearly indicates a hidden problem in the nature of psychoanalysis) has been an important stimulus to my thinking. I believe that it is relevant to the failure to describe the analytic process as it is really experienced that I have already mentioned. It is not surprising that my first scientific paper was concerned with the attempt to bring theory and practice together.

This was "The Structure of the Psychoanalytic Session,"

which I read at the first precongress scientific program in London in 1961 (see chapter 5). It was really my attempt to find an objective method in pychoanalysis which would be more logically analytical than the subjectivism, as it seemed to me, with which many analysts tended to react to their patients' material. It was as though they felt that there were some incompatibility between the logic of psychoanalysis and the release of inhibition in the analyst's use of free-floating attention and free association. The paper was designed to help a puzzled analyst to apply Freud's metapsychological concepts systematically to the details of a session and to construct from this study a model of the balance of forces at work in the session and in the patient's life. It seemed to me that too often the patient's fantasies were understood but the role of the ego, which gave them their significance, neglected. It is a startling comment on psychoanalytic training that the systematic application of existing concepts to a session seems to have struck a number of members of this international audience, not as banal but as containing something novel. The paper resulted in invitations to speak or publish abroad. As it scarcely ranks as an original contribution, this implies a criticism of our failure to come to grips with the problem of why metapsychology could not be successfully taught or could be taught only with great difficulty. I believe that a subsidiary reason why psychoanalytic teaching is frequently felt by students to be unsatisfactory is that the appeal to impulse contained in free association seduces teachers, who have themselves been capable of academic success in other fields, to abandon systematization. The paper's publication here represents its first appearance in English. I have always felt it to be too much a summary of accepted views to dare to submit it to an English journal.

But it was clearly its simplicity that recommended it to the audience. Its date already gives a lot of information about the difficulties of the psychoanalytic life. By 1961 I had been a full-time psychoanalyst for more than eight years, and all I had achieved was a certain mastery of basic technique. I could see what I was doing and teach it to others quite well. I was like a middle-grade doctor in a teaching hospital who often helps medical students more than a consultant. That is to say, I was still learning with an unquestioning faith in the theoretical system, and I could help others because I was being helped myself by my efforts to integrate my new understanding into my practice.

It seems to me that there are three main reasons why it proves such a hard task to integrate the Freudian metapsychology into clinical thinking. The first is the nature of its subject matter, to which I refer at various points, notably in "On the Dual Use of Historical and Scientific Method in Psychoanalysis" (see appendix A). The theories were developed in order to explain the clinical phenomena, but the clinical phenomena are complex and overdetermined. And the history of controversy from the beginning of psychoanalysis indicates that to reach even a clinical explanatory hypothesis which could be generally agreed upon was a formidable task. Even a group of modern psychoanalysts with considerable theoretical cohesion displays divergence of opinion when clinical material is discussed.

Secondly, any system which lays down broad conceptual categories to deal with the immense subtlety of human experience must fall short, however impressive its achievement. There is a gap between the conceptual categories of a metalanguage and the complexity of the actual psychic operations described in case reports. The metapsychological explanations show a preference for undifferentiated forces, such as drives or mental agencies, whereas the subtleties of

clinical practice are concerned with the individual's feelings
and values. If many psychoanalysts find it as difficult as they
do to use the language and concepts available, this does not
mean that they are unworthy of the language; it means that
the language, in spite of its achievement, is nonetheless in
some ways inadequate for them. It has to be recognized that
even the greatest achievement has its limits and that we
should be careful not to allow metapsychological rigor to
inhibit thought as well as to facilitate it. Preoccupation with
metapsychology may bias the analyst toward categories of
explanation which may sometimes be rooted as much in the
revolutionary nature of Freudian discoveries as in the actual
transformations which psychoanalysis can effect in a particular patient. This problem is discussed in "Formulating Interpretations in Clinical Psychoanalysis" (see chapter 7). Many
analysts clearly feel oppressed by concepts they cannot handle
and become afraid of their own originality.

To explain clinical phenomena was never the sole purpose
of Freud's theories. They were to provide a psychology for
neurologists, an account of the workings of the mental
apparatus, a psychology of the dream process, even ultimately an insight into the mode of operation of the forces of
life and death. Those concepts which are basic to clinical
work, such as the theory of unconscious mental processes,
displacement, condensation or repression command a very
high degree of agreement. As soon as a step is taken into
metapsychology consent diminishes: for instance, the concept
of psychic energy, which is generally considered essential to
explain such phenomena as displacement, comes under peri-
odic attack. As the concepts become more complex and less
obviously close to clinical experience, their necessity as
modes of explanation becomes less compelling. It is not
always easy to agree on what derives from the id, or from the

ego, or to define the area of operation of the superego, let alone the degree of fusion or defusion of the drives.

This leads to the third reason why the Freudian meta-psychology is difficult to assimilate. It represents more than simply the clinical discoveries of a great man; it also expresses his philosophy and the philosophy of his age. This raises the problem of how and in what conditions we can integrate into ourselves not so much the discoveries as the points of view of a great man and still keep our own personalities and derive pleasure from our creativity. The older analysts were able to do this more easily because of their personal bond with a living master. But to develop, it is necessary to liberate ourselves from our parents, our analysts, and our teachers. The mantle of an Elijah does not fall easily on another individual, and indeed Old Testament scholars have concluded that Elisha was a much inferior type of prophet.

In writing "The Structure of the Session" I was expressing my feeling that I now had a reasonable understanding of Freud's thought. This gave me the confidence to try to move on. The next paper, "A Particular Form of Transference in Neurotic Depression" (see chapter 6), tried basically to expand the formula of "The Structure of the Session" to accommodate some common elements in the psychology of a new type of patient who was said to be coming to analysis since the war—patients whose main complaint was depression. It approached the problem from the point of view of the ego psychology which so much influenced psychoanalytical thought at the time, but it attempted to do so in a way which described the processes of the ego in strictly clinical terms with recourse to as few clichés as possible. The personal importance of this becomes clearer if one remembers that a comparatively junior member of the British Society in the sixties, striving for an independent view of psychoanalysis, was liable to feel himself fighting a war on two fronts. One aim was to understand and yet not be overwhelmed by the formidable conceptual sophistication, the refinement of developmental theory, and the systematic approach to therapy of the conservative forces. The other was to appreciate the increased subtlety and range introduced into the psychoanalytical relationship by the Kleinian appreciation of the role of early affects and by their ability to explore them in the transference. This appreciation had to be accomplished in the face of the reserve generated by an emphasis on the importance of inborn or early-acquired characteristics which seemed not to fit easily with common experience. Melanie Klein's writings acknowledge the influence of the parents, if somewhat vaguely. In practice their role was much less stressed in clinical presentations before Bion's concept of the mother as a container was taken up increasingly in the 1960s. Influences on the child after it had negotiated the depressive position at six to eight months had seemed to count for very little, though this may have been due in some measure to the need to emphasize what was new in the Kleinian point of view. Yet the psychological processes which Klein described, shorn of their developmental timetable, seemed often to be an important advance, notably the psychology of the depressive position, the descriptions of the interplay of primitive defense mechanisms such as projective identification and splitting, and even the psychology of unconscious envy, if it were not regarded as innate. In the paper on the depressive transference I tried to build my own picture of what had happened in my patients' development, influenced by Melanie Klein's emphasis on internalization processes, but not losing contact with classical metapsychology. I tried to describe the external influences operating on the child as reconstructed from his object relationships inside and outside the analysis, and from his history and the way in which pregenital attitudes could be condensed with phallic impulses in the oedipal phase to form the fantasies that determine life and character. I tried particularly to show the way in which the depressive constellation and its resolution were reflected in various stages of the transference. Many of these aspirations were not conscious at the time; I simply wanted to formulate some statement which would help me to find a psychoanalytical identity.

There is another element which was beginning to emerge. The paper describes three stages, that is, a process. In this it was strongly influenced by the classical concept of the gradual release of warded-off material into consciousness as defenses are undone. But I was also becoming aware that this process could be interfered with and that what was sometimes classed as the patient's resistance could be provoked by the analyst, that is, of the extent to which psychoanalysis is a reciprocal process in which the personal feelings of analyst and patient to one another, which were often not expressed, could play an important role. I think that my emphasis on the nature of the unexpressed relationship between analyst and patient was also in part a product of the controversies of the time. It was my commentary on the seeming inability of protagonists of either theoretical viewpoint to identify the merits and demerits of each method and its areas of therapeutic applicability. In this I was too harsh: the refined assessment of results in psychoanalysis presents insuperable logical difficulties. But it was true that concentration on the method ignored the personal factor, though in fact the personal factor is central to the method. It determines what the analyst selects for interpretation, in what way he views what he selects, and even perhaps to some extent what the patient brings. If the number of requests for a paper is any guide for the need to emphasize this point of view, then it is of interest

that the expansion of this theme in 1968 in "The Psychoanalyst as a Person" (see chapter 8) proved by far the most
popular paper I have written.

The paper "Reporting Dreams in Psychoanalysis" (see
chapter 1) arose from a seemingly irrational inner conviction,
but it was also in part stimulated by the failure of two schools
of psychoanalysts to define each other's point of view and
answer it effectively. The Kleinians were often criticized for
interpreting the manifest content of a dream without reference to any associations—a criticism which they rejected.
But it was easy to observe that analysts of all opinions seemed
sometimes to interpret the manifest content directly. The
argument, as I later realized, depended on what one regarded
as associations, which was not uniform in any group. I began
to become aware of a dichotomy between teaching and
practice which was more fundamental than a difference
between schools. Though everyone taught the Freudian theory of the dream as an attempted wish fulfillment, I noticed
that it was quite rare for the wish in a dream actually to be
interpreted. My paper is based on the theory that the dream is
a wish. But it also tries to enter the area of the metapsychological gap by describing the way in which a patient can
allow primary and secondary processes to interpenetrate one
another in an attempt, with the analyst's help, to find a
solution to his wishes in life. It then endeavors to consider the
special role of dreams in the psychic life and why they have in
all ages been believed to foretell the future. In summary, it
turns from the function of the dream as an instinctual discharge phenomenon to the creative purposes of the dream in
analysis and in life. In this way it also adumbrates a certain
change in technique, restoring to the dream some of the
central role which it possessed in the earlier history of
analysis.

It seemed that some of the controversy over dream interpretation could be resolved if the distinction between two
classes of unconscious phenomena were kept clear. The first
class consists of interpretations of the unconscious proper,
which always impresses one, as Freud said in 1915, by its
profoundly irrational character. It derives this quality from
the characteristics of the System Unconscious. The second
class relates to the unconscious operations of the ego and to
the compromises which it tries to work out at various levels in
the preconscious. These interpretations do not impress us
with their irrational character. They are bound up with the
analysis of defense, but they interpret much more than
defense. They impress us with the patient's far-reaching
mental and emotional subtlety and with the abilities and
limitations he has at his disposal in finding a satisfactory
pathway in life. I have thought that a certain failure to
appreciate the validity of each type of interpretation lay
behind some of the criticisms which each school leveled at the
other. Technically I became convinced that if the implications of a dream in the context of the patient's life were to be
fully understood it was normally desirable to have his real
free associations and not his forced free associations. That is
to say, the dream needs to be studied as it occurs spontaneously in the context of the session. If the analyst asks the
patient for associations he stops him in his spontaneous
associations in order to replace them with forced associations
in accordance with a technical model dating from the time
when psychoanalysis was in its infancy. I became convinced
that nothing essential is lost by accepting the patient's free
associations without interference; there is no need to fall into
any trap of making superficial interpretations from the manifest content only. Indeed the interpretations seemed to be far
richer and more fully relevant to the patient's life problems

when they could be easily connected with all that occurred in the session and with the transference. Almost the only exception to this is where the patient's spontaneous communication fails. I believe that I learned this from one variety of Kleinian technique, though I cannot be sure that my formulation of it would be acceptable to Kleinian analysts. However, my interpretations emphasize more (or so it seems to me) the point at which unconscious fantasies crystallize to determine the patterns of life and less the interplay of primitive defenses than those of most Kleinians.

Reading the paper again, after more than ten years, I am impressed by how portentous the two short dreams were for both patients—more than I knew at the time. This raises the question of whether I selected these dreams, which have a certain similarity in form and content, because I appreciated their significance unconsciously or whether all dreams are as rich in content if only one could understand them. I will attempt a partial answer. I underestimated what dreams can yield when I said in the paper that we often understand little or nothing of them, or perhaps only a fragment of defense. Writing it alerted me—or was probably the expression of my becoming alert—to how much one can get from a dream if one regards it as expressing the core of the session when seen in relation to the transference, that is, as lying at the junction of the two royal roads to the unconscious. This is where what is symbolized in the dream is repeated in interpersonal terms. It is where id and ego come together, giving the dream its special brilliance. Of course one does not get the same amount from every dream. Many factors influence this in terms of the readiness of patient and analyst to communicate with one another. But once the analyst has understood the patient's dream, one can see in how many different ways he repeats it and clarifies it in his associations, his relationship to the analyst, and his life. One can understand why the ancients thought that dreams came from the gods.

With the publication of the paper on dreams, I must have felt in a position to formulate some general attitudes to psychoanalysis, both as a clinical endeavor and as a theory. This summing up is contained in the papers "Personal Attitudes to Psychoanalytic Consultation" (see chapter 9) and "On the Dual Use of Historical and Scientific Method" (see appendix A). In the first of them I emphasized the important prognostic significance of the power of analyst and patient to engage with one another, and I adopted a note of caution against (perhaps) "the widening scope of psychoanalysis" when such a major procedure seemed often to be undertaken too lightly, and so many analyses lasted so long with benefits which sometimes did not seem commensurate. In the theoretical paper I considered what the logic of our method really is—how much is scientific in that it leads to the description of the regularities known as scientific "laws" and how much depends on complex acts of historical assessment of an individual character. I do not think that I need to make further comment on these papers.

But problems of the logic of the theory and practice of psychoanalysis would not leave me alone. There was not only the problem of the two groups of analysts in the British Society (with the largest group not taking sides, it is true, but not appearing to be outstandingly successful in clarifying the problems either). There was also the problem of the mechanism of cure, and within this, of the resolution of the transference and countertransference. Indeed the failure to resolve the logic of the mechanism of cure was obviously responsible for some of the difficulties. How could two groups of analysts both claim successes by methods which the other group questioned? I felt uncomfortable at the attitude of analysts of every group in relation to cure. I was surprised, for instance, by the extent to which recommendations to a particular analyst seemed to depend upon results rather than method. I felt uneasy at such remarks as "The patient got better, so he must have understood him," or "He must be getting something out of it if he keeps coming." What was the patient getting out of it, and what was happening in all those cures to which analysts seemed to shut their eyes (or to dismiss) brought about by innumerable other methods of treatment, or even by Christian Science? Clearly psychoanalysis needed to have something more capable of definition in its mechanisms of cure. What was due to general factors which applied to other therapies, and what was specific to psychoanalysis and depended on its method? How much did we interpret for the benefit of the patient, and how much for our own satisfaction? I knew I could not solve these problems, but in 1972 I wrote an exploratory article "On the Relationship of Transference and Interpretation in Psychoanalytic Therapy" (see chapter 2).

The paper achieved a good response, but I am now better able to add to it from the standpoint of ego psychology. In 1974 Nicole Berry published an important paper—"From Fantasy to Reality in the Transference (or The Double Aspect of the Psychoanalyst)." In it she distinguished between the analysis of the patient's fantasies and the recognition of his personality. It seems to me profitable to consider some aspects of the transference from the point of view of "recognition." The psychoanalytic method is in fact designed to produce confusion in the patient as well as a sense of being recognized—a confusion which it seeks only gradually to resolve. This is the confusion over which of the patient's instinctual objects is current and which archaic, and it is manifested in the development of transference. It is the making visible of this confusion that is intended to resolve it. But it is essential to distinguish the forces making for confusion from those making for its resolution. What first attracts the patient to the psychoanalyst, for instance, is certainly not a sexual experience. It is the experience of being recognized. It is in gratitude for this that love comes, and with it—slowly—sexuality. What signals recognition are first the analyst's attention and then the responsiveness and understanding conveyed in his interpretations. But it takes time for the analyst to understand, and during this time (whether long or short) the analyst withholds the clues to his response. The fact that the patient begins a flight from reality in which he substitutes ingrained images from childhood for the analyst is evidence that his mind cannot stand the strain of the relationship. Basically he attempts to supply himself with the image of the early mother who satisfied in compensation for that of the analyst, who frustrates (though it may sometimes seem the other way round). These two images, one from the present, one from the past, cannot be held separate for an indefinite time. The longings that recognition stirs are too primitive: the mother's first response to her baby is rather surprisingly but significantly called "recognition behavior," and to be recognized is a fundamental human need. The images therefore become confused—in psychoanalytic language they are condensed. The System Unconscious, which can appreciate likenesses but cannot discriminate, has taken over. The task of analysis is then to use the discriminating power of the ego to study a greater range of likenesses that would otherwise have been available and to differentiate one from another.

While the experience of recognition is paramount, the patient responds in a way which is difficult to describe. It is often said that he falls in love with the analyst or that there is a honeymoon period. This leaves out the fact that he probably has at this stage little sexual interest in the analyst. What he experiences should probably be compared only to the earliest stages of falling in love in which Freud noted the characteristic inhibition of sexuality—accepting the analyst with his feelings, revering him and enjoying his presence as a small child might. Adult sexuality becomes intensified when the analyst becomes more realistically human, more equal, and therefore more easily also the object of aggression. Typically analysis repeats the development of the child. The oedipus complex, maturationally programmed, also arises in analysis with psychological maturation, and it is as a result of this that it appears most strongly in the transference—or so I have found. It can of course be interpreted from the beginning and often must be—for instance when jealousy plays an important part in the precipitation of the illness—but in my view, if it is interpreted too early something more basic is usually missed.

The powerful longings that cause the patient's confusion put the analyst to some extent in the position of the sorcerer's apprentice. The confusion is by no means always fully resolved. I believe that the length of time that it takes so many analysts to form their own view of psychoanalysis is partly due to the confusion that they have experienced in their own analysis and the fact that its resolution is made more difficult by the continuation of the transference in the professional tie.

The psychoanalyst's emotional dependence on his patient is clearly different but not as dissimilar as it might first appear. He does not normally experience the patient's libidinal thralldom, though he may have favorites and can certainly experience the sense of loss. But he has to struggle against a longing to be recognized by his patients, which may distort his judgment and feed his vanity, and therefore, since it is a failure in his analytic work, ultimately feed his depression.

He too needs interpretation to deeroticize his relationships—often provided in effect by discussion with colleagues. But analysts seem to me in general to deny the influence that their patients have on them. Perhaps they invest the analytic process with some of their frustrated libido. The result may well be an area of confusion in which analysts find it difficult to assess psychoanalysis because they have idealized it. These remarks expand a line of thought which I brought forward in 1976 in "Some Little-Described Elements of the Psychoanalytical Relationship" (see chapter 3), which considered the analytical process more from the point of view of relationship than "Transference and Interpretation" and less from that of instinctual regression.

My views were summarized and added to in the paper on the "Identity of the Psychoanalyst" (see chapter 10), which opened the discussion at the Haslemere Conference on this theme, arranged by the International Psychoanalytical Association in 1976. One more paper fits with the last three mentioned. This is the paper on "Analyses That Cannot Be Terminated" (see chapter 4). The more importance one attributes to early object relationships which cannot be resolved and the more one appreciates that termination involves trauma, the more difficult it becomes to impose a termination on the patient. Patients must choose their own time, and the process of analysis cannot be hurried. There remain a few patients—in my experience very few—who cannot internalize the analytical process to a degree that enables them to become independent. That is to say, psychoanalysis has its limitations, and in such cases the patient's dependency has to be accepted in some degree. But even in these cases the patient wishes to regain his independence and usually gradually does so.

I have not referred to all my papers and not yet to my paper on religion (see appendix B), but it is germane to my attitude to psychoanalysis, which I should now like to describe. The thesis of this paper is that religion has to assert as truth things which it is impossible to believe because such an assertion is the only means of affirming early experience which seems incredible. The truth of religion lies in the experiences it reaches by means of its symbolism. I became a psychoanalyst as an act of faith in the truth enshrined in it, and therefore, in this limited sense, psychoanalysis could be called my religion. But if we have to assert its literal truth defensively or preserve every opinion that Freud expressed, then we come to share the less attractive aspects of other western religions: a messianic approach with elements of creed and dogma and a tendency to turn a blind eye to uncomfortable facts. Much of what I have written, especially in more recent papers, has been a reaction against this aspect of psychoanalysis as I have experienced it. Perhaps my feelings are exaggerated, but there have always been analysts who have been disturbed by a tendency to make psychoanalysis, or a form of psycho-analysis, into a cult. Where psychoanalysis should differ from other religions—as on the whole it does—is in allowing what is false in it to be more easily exposed, instead of insisting on its affirmation as proof of social and psychological reliability.

I

Difficulties in the Therapeutic Situation

1

Reporting Dreams in Psychoanalysis (1967)

Why patients report dreams on one day and not on another is a question which does not seem to have been asked before in the psychoanalytic literature. The answer is that a repressed wish has come near enough to consciousness to demand a solution in life. To report a dream means that the patient is seeking the analyst's help in integrating the conflict between psychic structures. It is because a repressed wish is seeking fulfillment that dreams in all ages have been regarded as foretelling the future.

A dream is a private work of art. Like all art it is, in Picasso's phrase, a fiction that brings us nearer reality.

* * *

3

No general explanation seems to have been achieved of why patients report their dreams on some occasions and not on others. It is true that we commonly refer the failure to report dreams, as we do the failure to suggest associations to them, to the patient's resistance, that is, to a disturbance as a result of anxiety of the synthetic function of the ego. The absence of a positive theory of the significance of reporting a dream is especially surprising when we consider that a dream has been regarded as an important psychic event throughout the history of mankind.* If the evidence of the literature were taken alone, dream interpretation might seem to have been the cornerstone of Freud's technique for as long as twelve years; but Freud discusses the psychology of the dream process and its relationship to the remembered fragment of the manifest content, rather than the psychology of reporting dreams and the question of why patients report them when they do. In 1913 Ferenczi referred, as though to a commonplace, to the psychoanalyst's knowledge that people tell their dreams to the person to whom their contents refer. If this also holds true of the fragment of the dream life reported in analysis, then its clinical implication would be that all dreams in analysis concern the psychoanalyst. Though many analysts regard all the phenomena of the session primarily from the standpoint of the transference, I do not recall any statement that all dreams in psychoanalysis refer directly to the analyst; for instance, Rosenbaum, in his paper "Dreams in Which the Analyst Appears Undisguised" (1965), drew only the cautious conclusion that dreams in which the analyst

*Since this paper was written, a further interesting contribution has been made by Martin S. Bergmann: "The Intrapsychic and Communicative Aspects of the Dream: Their Role in Psychoanalysis and Psychotherapy" which includes a review of changing attitudes toward the dream from ancient times.

appears undisguised in the manifest content may well be concerned with an aspect of the patient's real relationship with him.

In recent years the operation of the ego in the dream process has been given increased recognition. In 1954 Erikson emphasized the reflection of the dreamer's total situation on every level of the manifest dream. Kanzer (1955) stressed the communicative function of the dream and offered a reconciliation of this function with the theory of the narcissism of sleep. Kris (1956) included the solution of problems in dreams as an example of the integrative work of the preconscious, and Lewin (1958) illustrated the constructive use of dream regression in the formulation of creative ideas. Examples of dreams selectively told to individuals who were less likely to understand them than the psychiatrist to whom they referred were cited by Whitman in 1963. The theory that dreams are to be understood essentially as problem-solving activities was put forward by French in 1954 and again by French and Fromm in 1966. However, the conceptual standpoint of French and Fromm appears to give a dynamic role to the ego which is not easily integrated with other psychoanalytic concepts.

There are few phenomena of analysis which can be relied on more consistently to arouse the interest and expectation of both patient and analyst than the patient's report of a dream. My aim in this paper is to suggest explanations for the high valuation accorded to the reporting of dreams in the light of modern psychoanalytic theory.

For instance, does this feeling of expectation in itself allow any conclusion to be drawn about the function of a dream— or, rather, of remembering and reporting a dream? Affects are regarded as responses of the ego, and Freud's view of 1900 that they are less plastic than ideation remains a fundamental postulate of psychoanalysis. An important step forward in the integration of metapsychology and technique was taken when Heimann drew attention, in her paper of 1950 "On Countertransference", to the importance of the analyst's affective reactions as indicators of the patient's unconscious mental processes. Whether one subscribes to her equation of the countertransference for the purposes of her paper with the totality of the analyst's responses, or prefers, like Little (1957), another designation, or, like Hoffer (1956), attempts some degree of distinction between appropriate and inappropriate responses by the analyst, a new source of clinical information was introduced and made respectable by her contribution, and a new dimension defined for the study of clinical interaction.

The evocation of the psychoanalyst's interest by the dream accords well with older as well as with newer theories. If a dream represents the attempted fulfillment of a repressed wish, it becomes comprehensible—in a sense almost axiomatic—that affect is stimulated in the analyst, though the mechanism of this process still lacks full definition. When we recall that for the first time there is a possibility that their dreams will be consciously understood, the fact that patients often recall dreams with greater facility in analysis also becomes comprehensible. Moreover, even remembered dreams from the past acquire a special significance as communications to the analyst and do so in different ways according to the phase of the analysis. It would seem justifiable to conclude that the evocation of the particular interest that accompanies the report of a dream indicates that a communication of particular importance is being attempted. Often, of course, we understand little, or nothing, of a dream, and it is forgotten. It is, however, also true that a dream of which little has been understood may remain with the analyst as a

recurring memory. I believe the theory that a special communication with the analyst is being attempted can be given
prima facie support. It seems usually to be possible to relate
significantly at least some fragment of the session to the
dream recounted—perhaps only a mode of defense, perhaps a
reference to a past event which will later emerge as a cover
memory, perhaps the foreshadowing of an impulse to be
expressed in action, but also, and not altogether rarely,
perhaps the clarification of the session's transference or of a
life problem.

To sum up, the patient's report of a dream may mean that
some new problem of communication with the analyst is
becoming acute. The partial breakthrough of a repressed
wish in a dream gives to the dreamer an urge to communicate
it, since impulses no longer under the full control of the ego
must seek discharge. The verbalization of the dream, like the
dream itself, represents a substitute discharge. With verbalization, this discharge is brought within the conditions of
object relationship and reality and no longer remains purely
endopsychic. What is added to the general conditions govern-
ing the report of a dream in the conditions of psychoanalysis is
an achievement by the ego of a new relationship to its
libidinal object, since, as has been indicated, for the first time
the dreamer has acquired the possibility of being consciously
understood.

If it is true that the report of a dream in analysis represents
a crisis in the attempt to make a new communication, then
this implies that some act of integration has been achieved by
the ego of elements of the id or superego, which were
previously inaccessible through defense. To formulate this
further, the report of something so structured as a dream may
indicate the mobilization of endopsychic conflict in such a
way that the ego attempts to define an acceptable attitude to

the conflict. This formulation would only be in line with the age-old view of mankind that dreams have a special meaning. Why this meaning has been held to be that of foretelling the future will be considered later.

I propose to examine two dreams in the light of this theory. The first has been chosen because it was the first dream of a patient who had spent some months in treatment without consciously dreaming. The transition to the reporting of dreams often illustrates the ego's achievement of a new capacity for integration very clearly. The only dream of this kind currently available to me was reported by a man, Mr. A, who had been in twice-weekly psychotherapy with me for about five months. (Geographical difficulties prevented his coming more often.) He sat in a chair, but, as far as these limitations allowed, my technique with him was analytic. Of working-class origin, conceived before marriage by an extravagant mother of bad sexual reputation and a father whom he suspected of having made her pregnant in order to secure her, he had made a remarkable success of his life. He had been unable to allow himself to capitalize his talents, however, until he was in his twenties. Recently he had been promoted managing director of a specialized engineering firm. He presented with complaints of panic attacks in situations in which it could be divined that the responsibilities of his new position weighed on him, and of anxiety for his future on their account. He told me that another psychiatrist had made a diagnosis of depression, but he was at a loss to understand either the precipitation or the meaning of his symptoms. He could list three events which his intellect told him might have had a connection with them. The first was his appointment as managing director three months before the full emergence of his symptoms. This had been "a body blow" to him because it meant that he replaced a superior who had helped him in his career and had recommended that he should succeed him when he himself was resigning owing to differences within the firm with which he was no longer willing to contend. Secondly, the appointment had involved a not very welcome move of his home and place of business and a great deal of overwork. Thirdly, his wife had reacted with unexpected hostility to finding herself pregnant for the third time after an interval of eight years, had vomited throughout the pregnancy, and, although she had previously opposed abortion for any woman in any circumstances, had repeatedly demanded that she herself be aborted. In fact she had borne the child, and her emotional state was "almost" back to normal. He regarded his marriage as exceptionally happy.

For several weeks before the dream, the patient had been telling me of his feelings as an eight- or ten-year-old when he had been left by his parents to look after the other children, including a baby sister, while they went out drinking. He described in particular his panic one night when the baby cried continuously and they had failed to return until late. He emphasized his mother's bad reputation both sexually and as a household manager and described in particular a row that his parents had had after his mother had disappeared from a pub and his father had found her at the back of it with a man. At the same time, he told me casually that his wife had had an affair with a friend of his not long before she became engaged to him—and indeed that one of the reasons that this affair had broken up was that his friend's parents had objected to her— but the only parallel he had drawn between his mother and his wife was that there was a definite similarity of physical appearance between them.

On his return from a business trip, he reported the following dream: He had been to a hotel and slept with the receptionist. A little while later he found that his friend had done the same. I did not interpret the dream to him in terms of his feelings about his wife, as I considered that her failure to accept their third child rendered his feelings of rejection by her too painful for my intervention. I therefore related my interpretation of the problem to its expression in the transference. I suggested that the dream referred to his anxiety over having missed sessions owing to his trip and to his jealousy over what other patients I might have been seeing in his hours. Two sessions later, however, he started the session by looking at me and smiling, and said "I'm beginning to see what all this is about." There followed an event which was rare in his marriage; he had a violent row with his wife over her insistence that on Sunday morning, instead of playing tennis, he should look after the children and allow her to sleep. This was followed by a reconciliation after a couple of days, but there was a decisive change in the type of his associations. Not only did he bring much more information about his wife's hysterical temperament and about his use of the withdrawal technique in sexual intercourse (more in accordance with his parents' social position and generation than with his own), but he started to report the fantasies which occurred to him about the consulting room—he saw bloodstains on the frame of the picture above the fireplace— and to speak much more freely about his feelings about me. He told me how he longed for a comfort from me which I refused him: for instance, I should say I was sorry for him and give him a prescription. At the same time, he said he was feeling better.

The second dream is also a short one, reported by a woman, Mrs. B, who had been coming at first four times, then five times a week for nine months. Since the death of her mother twelve years before, this patient had listened to her voice every day in her imagination, discussing the details of her life with her and tending to remonstrate with her. During the same period the patient had quarreled increasingly with her husband, whereas previously she had got on well with her husband and quarreled with her mother. The analysis had begun when she moved to London. She had undertaken it in an effort to save the marriage and decided that she must give up her lover of three years' standing with whom she had for the first time experienced sexual satisfaction. She had just returned from a seaside holiday. Her husband had pleased her by spending a few days with her and the children. She reported that during the holiday she had had the following dream: The stone of a gold ring like her mother's was dropped and was lost in the sand.

I have assumed that the capacity to report a dream in analysis indicates that the ego is attempting to formulate an attitude to the underlying conflict. More accurately, the report of a dream indicates an abortive attempt by the synthetic function of the ego to integrate the psychic structures. The ego, which cannot formulate its thought according to the reality principle, is endeavoring to formulate it by a mixture of primary and secondary processes in an attempt to communicate with the analyst and obtain his assistance. If this is so, the ego's statement will be concerned with the patient's current reality, with his relationship to the analyst, and also, since the dream is the attempt to fulfill a wish, with his relationship to the future.

In Mr. A's dream of the hotel receptionist, these elements were almost manifest. The dream portrayed some of his reflections on the repetition of his childhood emotions of disappointment and suspicion in his relationship with his wife and with me and adumbrated an acceptance of his resentments and a reevaluation, on the whole favorable to her, of his wife's character. At the same time, his increased freedom of communication showed an increased trust in me.

I should like to examine in greater detail Mrs. B's dream of
the stone of a ring being dropped. At the time of telling me
the dream, Mrs. B had an immediate dread: her sister was
coming on a visit. Her sister invariably quarreled with her,
trying to undermine her confidence in herself and in the way
she arranged her life. Her particular concern was to conceal
from her that she still had a lover. She told me how proud
Mrs. B's mother had always been of her as opposed to her
sister and how her mother had always loved to show her off.
In fact, I interpreted, how she had always been her mother's
gem. But how frustrated, Mrs. B went on, she had always
been by her mother's perpetual habit of keeping her waiting
or of having her nose in a book. That is to say, Mrs. B as a
child had been the stone that was displayed but also lost. Mrs.
B had told me of an anxiety attack she had once had when left
waiting in the street for her mother. In other words, the
dream crystallized Mrs. B's unconscious realization that she
might not be the stone firmly set in her mother's ring, or
indeed the only pebble on the beach in relation to her
husband, who also perpetually kept her waiting, especially by
not coming home from the office until late in the evening.
This she tried to deny both with her first associations about
her mother's pride in her and, subsequently, by acting in the
transference relationship. She had told me that her lover
intended to visit her but had not presented this as imminent.
The next day my receptionist reported that Mrs. B had
telephoned with a short message that she was unable to come
for two days. She had therefore suddenly dropped out of my
ring. On the third day, she telephoned me to say that although
she had intended to come, she did not think it would be
possible to get back in time after seeing her lover off at the
airport. Something in her manner made me ask what time the
plane left, and I could show her that she could, in fact, get

back in time. I was forced in this way to show her that I valued her, that she was my gem who had been lost and found again, in spite of her illicit absence with her lover. On her return, she told me that she was ill, her lover was a tranquilizer. She had just heard that her elder daughter was bottom of the class, and she feared that she had passed on to this daughter her own difficulty in adapting.

The attempted formulation in the dream could now be better understood. It was that her dependent relationship with her mother, as displayed in her symptom of listening to her voice, covered an essential incompatibility; that she could not deal with her ambivalence either by her attempts to deny her husband's neglect of her and interest in other women or by her idealization of her relationship with her lover. She showed the same struggle in relation to me by acting out and by the oscillation between listening to me with bated breath and the inability to accept the slightest frustration of her material demands on me which characterized the months that followed. The dream also hinted at an incipient realization that it was her jealousy of her sister that had caused her to form such a relationship of hostile dependency with her mother. This attempted formulation by the ego proved to contain a correct estimate of her future relations with her husband. Some weeks later she again saw her lover, with great precautions for concealment. But immediately afterward her husband announced his intention of leaving her, and she replied by begging him to stay. It gradually emerged that he himself had a mistress, who was imposing her claims on him. It seems that her dream had expressed her unconscious realization, or at least her fear based upon realistic assessment, that she was the stone that had been dropped from the marriage ring and would be lost in the sand of her disrupted life and obsessional personality.

With the partial exception of the reconstruction of past events, there is no critical method for validating hypotheses in psychoanalysis. It is an inevitable consequence of the complex overdetermination of psychic phenomena that a variety of explanatory concepts can be employed to account for them. This is one of the reasons why psychoanalytic findings, as Gillespie once pointed out, are more frequently confirmed than they are refuted. In this instance, agreement that the dreamer's preconscious impressions may become more accessible to the reality ego in dream crises does not of necessity imply that all dreams are attempts of the synthetic function to integrate the structures. Nonetheless, in the words of Novalis, quoted by Popper as an introduction to *The Logic of Scientific Discovery*, "Theories are nets: only he who casts will catch." I will bring forward eight metapsychological propositions which make some attempt to conceptualize the significance of reporting dreams as a clinical phenomenon. I shall then sketch some technical corollaries.

1. *The report of a dream in psychoanalysis indicates that the existence of a conflict is impinging on the conscious and preconscious systems.*

Mr. A had spoken for several weeks of how abandoned he had felt by his parents, laying the blame on the flightiness of his attractive mother whom his father had struggled to control. He had been overburdened by the responsibilities which had been heaped on him as a child, and he had been telling me for months of his panic attacks which had first appeared in connection with the social and psychic consequences of his new position at work. The reconstruction of his childhood feeling that he was an unwanted child was followed by his first dream. The partial interpretation of the dream in the transference brought to consciousness the realization that his relationship with his wife was troubled in a similar way by his feelings of being unappreciated by her and by an underlying distrust. In the second example, Mrs. B's dream gave a clear indication that she realized unconsciously that her husband intended to leave her long before she could bring herself to admit it consciously. Her conscious fear at the time of the dream was that she might have to leave her husband, whom she saw as sexually incapable, but wedded to his business, partly as a result of this. Mrs. B's dream was one which gave evidence, to use Freud's words. But the evidence that it gave was unlike that of the nurse's dream, which gave disguised expression to the confession that she had fallen asleep. The evidence to which Mrs. B's dream gave expression was not in consciousness. It was of the ego's awareness at an unconscious level of her fundamental unacceptability to her husband, as to her mother, which her symptom of listening to her mother's voice sought to deny.

The next proposition follows from this.

2. *To report a dream in analysis implies increased confidence in the power of the ego to stand conflict without resorting to rigid defenses.*

The latent content of a dream may be conceptualized under two categories. One is that of the latent wishes—the clothes-line, so to speak, from which all the derivatives of the id impulse hang. The second category is that of the unconscious and preconscious reactions of the ego to the incompatible elements from the id or primitive superego—more accurately, the reflections of the ego upon these elements at various levels of consciousness. I have maintained that when the patient brings a dream he expresses the hope that with the assistance of the analyst he may be able to integrate these incompatible derivatives into an acceptable attitude of the ego. The emergence of a manifest content indicates not only the defensive operations of the ego but also its willingness to give expression to these derivatives and to communicate them. Support for this view may be derived from Freud's statement that the emergence of a wish that has been interpreted into the manifest content of a subsequent dream may in general be taken as a confirmation of the interpretation. Perhaps the phenomenon of secondary revision may in part be understood in the same way, since it strives to integrate the logically incompatible elements of the dream into an acceptable story. The report of a dream represents not merely the attempt to form a compromise in ideation between ego and id; it also represents the increased confidence of the patient that he can achieve such a compromise in life.

3. *The report of a dream indicates that there is a barrier against the integration of the psychic structures.*

If there were no barrier, there would be no dream, but an attitude of the ego which could be verbalized. But the barrier may not be solely against an unacceptable impulse of the id or primitive superego. It may also have its origin in the patient's value system. Mrs. B's regression to a dependent relationship with her mother expressed not only her orality and homosexuality but also her pain at not having been able in reality to achieve the ideals set by her mother in independence from her. When she later acted out the latent thoughts and manifest content of her dream by making an attempt to jump from the balcony of her seventh-floor flat, (the stone dropping from the ring), she did so not only because her hatred of her mother (now of her husband) and her early fantasies of its consequences were impossible for her to integrate, but because of the sense of hopelessness induced by the incapacity of her ego to achieve its ideal. I do not wish to question the complexity of motivation in such an act or the role of fixation of the id in the helplessness of the personality. Mrs. B's

symptom of listening to her mother's voice testified sufficiently to her incapacity to master her oral destructive
fantasies. What I wish to suggest is that the economic
determinant of the barrier against integration can lie in those
affective processes of the ego which result from unconscious
thoughts in the secondary process reflecting on the derivatives of the id and drawing conclusions for the life pattern,
rather than simply in the anxiety produced by a regressive
drive. I would suggest further that the belief that dreams
foretell the future stems only partly from the unconscious
recognition that they express id derivatives which may seek
increasing discharge. It seems to me to stem also, as in this
dream, from the secondary processes which preconsciously
formulate an attitude to these derivatives in the light of the
ego's awareness of the limits of the personality consequent on
the fixations of the id and the distortions of the ego and
superego.

4. *The report of a dream indicates the operation of nonadaptive defense
mechanisms.*

Adaptive defense requires the neutralization of unacceptable id impulses and their displacement onto present objects.
The fact of distortion indicates that an attempt at neutralization is being made, but that it has failed. In the two dreams
reported, the attempt at neutralization is also evident in the
concentration of both of them upon an intellectual problem.
Mr. A's dream about the hotel receptionist openly expressed
a problem connected with the reevaluation of a personality
and attempted to visualize a nagging sore in his relationship
with his wife in wider terms of the general human problems
of sexual relationship. In Mrs. B's dream the affectively
agitating problem of where she will be able to find a life is
replaced by the intellectual problem "Where can I find the

stone?" But it is clear that successful neutralization would result in the ability of the ego to seek a new object, not in the continued fixation to a situation which seemed realistically to be untenable. The proposition that an attempt at neutralization has been made, but has failed, is a statement in the economic terms of ego psychology which complements the assertion that the manifest content of a dream represents a successful compromise formed by the dynamic interplay of ego and id.

5. *The titillation of the interest of both patient and analyst when the patient reports a dream indicates that crude energies are being allied with the neutralized energies.*

A change has occurred in the reservoir and flux of crude energy, so that the objects of displacement acquire a new excitement. Such a formulation follows Kris's illumination of the problem of sublimation. The increase in affective response of both patient and analyst indicates a change in economic factors comparable to that in sublimation, in which, as Kris showed, crude energies may play a considerable part. The arousal of interest indicates that a new pathway has been opened up for the cathexis of objects by the id. In Freud's psychology the mechanism of dream formation and of symptom formation are comparable. It is here suggested that the very different response of the patient, of the analyst, and indeed of the outside world, to the communication of a dream and of a symptom implies that a different balance has been achieved in the energy cathexes of the two. On the whole, the affect of the dreamer and of the listener to a dream, especially if the listener is a psychoanalyst, is one of hope. By contrast, a patient has to overcome a sense of shame in order to communicate a symptom, and in this case the affect of the outside world is suffused with fear, and that of the psychoanalyst with concern or with disquiet (in addition to his professional interest). There are, of course, disquieting dreams too, but there is a greater readiness to communicate them although they are by no means less comprehensible. Indeed, mankind has always felt that it had some understanding of the psychology of dreams, whereas the meaning of symptoms has tended to be a mystery usually requiring some degree of organic explanation. The spontaneous interest in dreams of patient and analyst indicates that at least a temporary success has been achieved in a reorganization of cathexes favoring the acceptable discharge of drive energy. In this way, the report of a dream becomes a member of a series which represents the freeing of energies that might otherwise be bound in symptom formation. It is in this sense that the aim of the patient's ego in reporting a dream may be compared to its aim in sublimation, a similarity recognized in modern artistic techniques which utilize a freer expression of primary process derivatives.

6. *The report of a dream indicates the patient's fear that the synthetic function of the ego may be paralyzed by primitive defenses.*

Proposition 2 maintained that the report of a dream implied an increase in the confidence of the ego. The present proposition is its antithesis and relates to the concomitant anxiety.

The cathexis of the perceptual system was related by Freud to the regressive defense against the stimulation of id impulses on the dream day. The cathexis of the perceptual system may also be taken to indicate that manifestations of the id are breaking through the defenses into the conscious and preconscious systems. But crude energies approaching consciousness have an urgency of drive which stimulates anxiety in the ego. This is the first reason why the report of a dream acquires a special psychic priority. Mr. A's dream heralded more than an increased ability to verbalize his dependency; my three subsequent holidays became periods of increased symptomatic distress for him, and two of them he was compelled to interrupt with the request that I should see him. Mrs. B's dream foreshadowed as a first consequence the presentation of her mourning in terms of an increased anal ambivalence toward me, expressed as difficulties over times and attendance. These were followed by her appreciation of the strength of her fears of soiling and their connection with her sexual inhibitions in marriage for which she now began to see that she might be paying the price. But when her unconscious knowledge that her husband intended to leave her was transformed into conscious knowledge by his statement of his immediate intention of doing so, her desire to be reunited with her mother and reborn, conceptualized in anal terms, broke through in a suicidal gesture. In spite of the dream, I had been unable sufficiently to work through her denials, and at least a partial paralysis of the synthetic function occurred. The report of the dream could be seen as an appeal to work with her in preventing the blurring through early defenses of the ego's capacity to evaluate.

7. *The access of crude energy to the ego gives dreams their prognostic significance.*

The release of crude energy confronts the ego with the problem of finding acceptable modes of discharge. The displacement that follows is therefore instigated as much by the secondary process as by the primary. The secondary process requires a search for substitutes of aim and object not linked with waking. Satisfactory substitutes can be found only in those memories or psychic equivalents, such as symbols, which are not dynamically or economically operative at the time of the dream. It is for this reason that repressed memories are cathected and unexpected symbolic equivalents suddenly illuminated. Dreams yield their clue to the psychic life because of the attraction of crude energy to details previously insignificant to the patient and often to the analyst. With Mr. A I could suspect in his casual reference to his wife's affair that its psychic consequences for him would prove important in the analysis. Mr. A himself appeared to have shrugged it off. It was not until the dream, followed by its interpretation in the transference, that he was able to speak of the pain it had caused him and to link it with his conviction of his wife's promiscuity as a girl which, when he confronted her with it, she seemed sincerely to repudiate as a fantasy. With Mrs. B the stone that dropped and was lost in the sand conveyed an affect which was immediately ominous, though it was some time before I could be convinced of the reality behind it since the patient continued insistently to deny it. Mrs. B played with object loss by acting out—taking extra holidays and suggesting that she reduce the number of sessions. She had told me that when her difficulties over her husband's neglect of her had first become acute she had had an impulse to jump out of the window and feared that it would return if her frustrations continued to be excessive. But she could not experience with any conviction the fear that her husband would leave her or that he might be having an affair with another woman. She could experience with full force, however, her affect in relation to her mother (though not to me), and her symptom of listening to her mother's voice had greatly diminished. It was the dream, however, and the gradual understanding of it, which deepened my sense of foreboding. The reason why mankind has always placed such a high estimation on the psychic significance of dreams may be because in these most nearly endopsychic phenomena the discharge of crude energy is most unrestricted by considerations of reality and object relationship. The reason why psychoanalysts estimate dreams so highly is that even in analysis, when dreams are communicated, the psychology of dreaming remains substantially unaltered.

8. *The integration of the latent dream thoughts into a manifest content which can be communicated indicates that the ego is attempting to integrate id derivatives in a form compatible with the demands of external reality and the mature superego.*

This proposition has already been adumbrated, but requires formal statement as a summary of the views I have presented concerning our interest in dreams in analysis. It stresses the operation of the synthetic function in the patient's achievement of communication. Perhaps this communication, like a joke, involves the sharing of guilt over the impulses which lie concealed beneath the manifest content. It may be from the resultant liberation that the ego derives an increased power to reflect realistically on the psychic situation. The portion of the vast total of regressive dreaming communicated in analysis may be that portion which the ego finds most adapted for the process of drawing new conclusions.

This theory is compatible with Freud's view of the manifest content as the product of the distortion of latent content by the operations of defense. If the ego is struggling to defend itself against the breakthrough of an incompatible id derivative, it may be regarded as part of the ego's aim to accept such representations of the id as it can in order to minimize conflict. The attempt of the ego to express an attitude to the id derivatives would only be its final achievement in the integration of defense and impulse.

I will end by summarizing the implications of these propositions for the theory of technique. Technically and economically the report of a dream indicates an irradiation of hidden areas of the psyche and thus offers a point of special attraction to the psychoanalyst. It is equally the irradiation of hidden areas—that is, the cathexis of nondynamic memories—which facilitates the expression of crude impulse. It is this expression, and the reflections of the ego upon its derivatives, which gives to the dream a prognostic significance. It is a corollary that a dream may need to be interpreted, not over one session alone, but over several, as its significance unfolds.

RERFERENCES

Bergmann, M.S. (1966). The intrapsychic and communicative aspects of the dream: their role in psychoanalysis and psychotherapy. *International Journal of Psycho-Analysis* 47:356-363.

Erikson, E. (1954). The dream specimen of psychoanalysis. *Journal of the American Psychoanalytic Association* 2:5-56.

Ferenczi, S. (1913). To whom does one relate one's dreams? In *Further Contributions to the Theory and Practice of Psycho-Analysis.* London: Hogarth, 1950.

French, T. M. (1954). *The Integration of Behavior: II. The Integrative Process in Dreams.* Chicago: University of Chicago Press.

French, T.M., and Fromm, E. (1964). *Dream Interpretation: A New Approach.* New York and London: Basic Books.

Freud, S. (1900). The interpretation of dreams. *Standard Edition* 4-5.

——— (1905). Jokes and their relation to the unconscious. *Standard Edition* 8.

——— (1913). An evidential dream. *Standard Edition* 12:267-277.

Heimann, P. (1950). On countertransference. *International Journal of Psycho-Analysis* 31:81-84.

Hoffer, W. (1956). Transference and transference neurosis. *International Journal of Psycho-Analysis* 37:332-333.

Kanzer, M. (1955). The communicative function of the dream. *International Journal of Psycho-Analysis* 36:260–266.

Kris, E. (1955). Neutralization and sublimation: observations in young children. *Psychoanalytic Study of the Child* 10:30–46.

——— (1956). Some vicissitudes of insight in psychoanalysis. *International Journal of Psycho-Analysis* 37:445–455.

Lewin, B.D. (1958). *Dreams and the Uses of Regression.* New York: International Universities Press.

Little, M. (1957). "R"—the analyst's total response to his patient's needs. *International Journal of Psycho-Analysis* 38:240–254.

Popper, Karl (1959). *The Logic of Scientific Discovery.* London: Hutchinson.

Rosenbaum, M. (1965). Dreams in which the analyst appears undisguised—a clinical and statistical study. *International Journal of Psycho-Analysis* 46.

Whitman, R. M. (1963). Remembering and forgetting dreams in psychoanalysis. *Journal of the American Psychoanalytic Association* 11:752–774.

2

The Relationship of Transference and Interpretation (1971)

This paper started with the puzzle presented by two schools of analysis in the British Society, each claiming superiority for its method. It had struck me increasingly that the importance of the personality of the analyst was minimized in the disputes over theory. In fact the disputes seemed to ignore many of the realities of the analytic interaction in favor of models which described analysis only at its best. The root of the paper lay in the tension between the schools, but its subject matter became the tension between analyst and patient, and the importance of interpretation in regulating it.

* * *

One of the earliest discoveries of psychoanalysis was that another factor was involved in therapy besides the interpretations of the analyst. This was the development by the patient of strong feelings of attachment. Freud came to appreciate the indispensability of such feelings, not only as a source of material for analytic interpretation but as a positive aid to treatment. In 1913 he recommended that the patient's positive transference should not be interpreted until it was used by him as a resistance.

Nonetheless, the total emphasis of Freud's view of psychoanalytic therapy was to stress the value of the capacity to understand, which was the essence of the psychoanalytic revolution. "Where id was, there shall ego be." Despite the usefulness of the patient's attachment to the analyst in inducing him to consider and accept interpretations, and as a source of material, its crude and infantile nature was such that transference was ultimately a resistance against analysis, whether it ostensibly took a libidinal or an aggressive form. Similarly countertransference was to be understood primarily as the analyst's unanalyzed resistance to the patient's material, and especially to his transference, requiring resolution by interpretation of its unconscious content.

I would like in this paper to present my own understanding of some trends in the development of the theory of transference and what is loosely called countertransference and to attempt some further formulations on their interplay with interpretation. I am, of course, aware that I can only make an approach to a most complex and difficult subject.

However much a psychoanalyst may wish to avoid Hartmann's "genetic fallacy" (1969) of equating the present with its origins, psychoanalytic psychology is a psychology of drives which are ultimately biological. It derives, as Bernfield (1932) showed with such clarity, from the school of

Helmholtz, embodied in Freud's teacher Brücke, whom he acknowledged as the most important intellectual influence in his life.

The technique of analysis in terms of biological drives inevitably has a "reductive" tendency, as was noted early by Jung. Skillfully given, reductive interpretations liberate by revealing the degree to which the impulses interpreted are egoalien and the creativity of which the ego is capable in making use of impulses, as in the richness of its choice of symbolism. This is especially evident in the analysis of symptoms. Crudely given to "explain" value systems, they tend to devalue the aspirations founded on them and provoke a sense of hopelessness. In practice the skill of the analyst is very much to be measured by his success in balancing these reductive implications by other features of psychoanalysis which make it liberating. He does this in a number of ways: by the moral qualities at his disposal for interest in the patient and identification with him; by showing the positive value of primitive mechanisms, as for example, when envy and oral incorporation are used for the ego's acquisition of new ideals; by the education in accepting the realities of the id which implicitly accompanies interpretation; by the analysis of current anxieties in everyday terms; and by the innumerable exchanges between patient and analyst which make the analytic experience a humane one. But these more complex elements in the interaction of patient and analyst, though portrayed in Freud's writings, have only slowly become the subject of theoretical discussion. They play little part in Freud's own treatment of the mechanism of psychoanalytic cure. Indeed he deprecated the frequent inquiries into the mechanism of cure which he considered to be sufficiently understood. In this attitude he was failing to apply the principles which he himself had discovered. He had shown that the persistence of doubt indicates that a problem remains.

I would like to start my discussion with Strachey's paper in 1934 on "The Nature of the Therapeutic Action of Psychoanalysis." This seems to me to represent a turning point. On the one hand, it represented the apotheosis of the Helmholtzian view of psychoanalytic therapy as the uncovering and resolution of forces latent in the patient, which then express themselves as "packets of id energy" directed toward the psychoanalyst. It was for this reason that the only possibility of "mutative" interpretation lay in interpreting the transference, and all other interpretations or therapeutic devices were a preparation for this. On the other hand, and in my opinion in uneasy juxtaposition with this way of thinking, the mutation came through the incorporation by the patient of the analyst's attitudes to the impulses into his superego. This was brought about by the analyst's capacity to interpret, and also to behave, in an objective manner when confronted by the patient's impulses. To my mind it is clear that this must involve the incorporation of aspects of his value systems which are in practice complex and individual.* In spite of Strachey's respect for the importance of the analyst's nonverbal behavior, which could result in an "implicit" mutative interpretation, he made it clear that the detailed interpretation of the patient's specific fantasies was in general essential.

Strachey's paper, with its emphasis on releasing latent forces in the transference, has had an immense influence on every psychoanalyst, and he presents a fairly convincing model of those phases of an analysis which are satisfactory to both patient and analyst. He does not present a convincing

---

*The study of patients who have previously been treated by another psychoanalyst reveals the enormous differences in moral and other value judgments between analysts.

picture of analysis "warts and all," and I believe that there are quite a few warts in most analyses. His paper in fact ends with unanswered questions concerning the analyst's inner difficulty in making interpretations, and it is here that it suggests the need for new approaches.

Strachey's model gives great importance to the analyst's technique of interpretation, carefully safeguarded by keeping his personality in the background as far as possible. While it represents an ideal of great heuristic value, it may be considered somewhat intimidating as a description of a clinical process. As Winnicott (1947) has pointed out, we all react differently to each one of our patients, so that it often happens that, in the words he once used in the British Psycho-Analytical Society, "the aim of analysis is to do standard analysis." He implied that when in these cases our capacity to interpret is at last functioning smoothly, we find that the patient is already on the way to being cured. That is a phenomenon which is not uncommon, but the patient's improvement seems difficult to explain on Strachey's hypothesis of the necessity of accurate and specific transference interpretation without some modification.

If therapeutic progress depends on the introjection of the analyst's value systems in relation to id impulses, these values have not been transmitted in this sort of case only by the detailed content of the analyst's interpretations in the transference, as the transference has been understood with great difficulty, and the interpretations have been inaccurate. The modification of the patient's superego must have been brought about by some form of unconscious communication: that is, by the "implicit" mutative interpretation which Strachey mentions. This hypothesis, however, needs further reconciliation with his general emphasis on the importance of detailed and specific interpretation.

The recognition that the transference-countertransference interaction between patient and analyst was considerably more complex has in fact gained ground increasingly since the time of Strachey's paper, and it has proved correspondingly difficult to limit the meanings of these terms by neat definitions. What appears in the literature as the most strikingly original contribution was perhaps Alice and Michael Balint's paper "On Transference and Counter-transference" in 1939, in which they drew attention to the fact that the analyst too has an emotional need to conduct his work in a way which suits his personality. They concluded, however, that with few exceptions the patient's transference evolved independently of the analyst's countertransference. Michael Balint has, however, not been slow to emphasize the corresponding factor in the operations of the analyst: that every analyst has his individual atmosphere, easily to be recognized. That is, his transference to his patients evolves to some extent in a set pattern determined by his own personality. One might surely add in a pattern determined by his own transference to his own analyst, and to psychoanalysis. It is interesting that Alice and Michael Balint stated as early as 1939 that the very possibility of the mirrorlike attitude recommended by Freud was being generally called into question. A second stage in the reconsideration of the classical view occurred after the war. This stage stressed the therapeutic importance of the analyst's response. In 1947 Winnicott emphasized in "Hate in the Countertransference" that the patient needed the reality of the analyst's emotions, which could be intense and negative, in order to appreciate the reality of his own personality. In 1950 Paula Heimann pointed out that the analyst's emotional response to his patient could be a valuable tool for understanding by empathy if it was properly controlled. For the first time countertransference became something more than a matter of the analyst's unresolved transference and resistance. A third stage, to which Searles and Racker were important contributors, recognized the frequency of a complex involvement between patient and analyst, while a fourth stage, not yet satisfactorily resolved, is characterized by the attempt to differentiate transference and nontransference elements in the relationship and to define "reality" in the analytic situation.

It seems to me that one of the difficulties in the theory of the therapeutic process has been a tendency to see it too much from the point of view of the content of interpretation at the expense of adequate study of the meaning of interpretation in the complex relationship of mutual transference. Charles Rycroft's paper in 1956 on "The Nature and Function of the Analyst's Communication to the Patient" was a notable exception.

The elements of the transference that have classically been interpreted have been the unsatisfied components of the patient's love impulses, his defenses against them, and his reactions to their frustration, particularly of aggression. The interpretation of these impulses also underlies much of the analysis of projection and introjection expressed in terms of the self, as Strachey tried to show with regard to the superego. Insofar as interpretation along these lines acts to hold the patient, it holds him by the affective satisfactions inherent in the resolution of conflict, by increasing his awareness of further conflict, and by the increased stimulation of his loving attachment to the analyst. But the nature of the actual loving attachment we are usually able to analyze only in comparatively crude and general terms which are highly dependent on reconstruction. What the patient expresses, whether overtly or unconsciously, is, in the context, largely fantasy, and this is already defensive. We can infer something of the general nature of the love impulses which hold the patient in analysis from the form that their disturbance takes—from anxiety over separation, from idealization or from later defenses against aggression, from oral attitudes toward interpretation, and so on, and from the nature of the latent hostilities. But the positive nature of the attachment—that part of our personalities and of the analytic process which revives the memories of the normal continuum of childhood, and what these memories are—with all this we often work largely in the dark. I think that these views are along somewhat similar lines to those Freud expressed in "Constructions in Analysis" (1937). Something similar can be seen when the patient comes for a second analysis with a new analyst; he is much better able to tell the new analyst what was wrong with his previous analysis than of the positive aspects which helped to hold him for the years it did. It is true that when we reconstruct the patient's affection for his parents he rewards us with memories. But these play a comparatively small part in an analysis dealing with disturbances and tend to come after the analysis of the defensive aggression.

My point is that the transferences which hold the patient to us are more easily analyzed in fairly crude, instinctual terms than in terms of the character attitudes and sympathies derived from the complex crystallization of fantasies for the most part in the phallic phase and in latency. Who always knows what makes an immediate sympathy between patient and analyst or a quickness of understanding (though we can analyze the opposite more easily)? It may depend, for instance, on an immediate unconscious appreciation of the areas of mutual vulnerability, not revealed, if at all, until a second analysis. Yet the nature of this unanalyzed transference must play a considerable part in the outcome. After all, the patient brings his associations to the analyst as a person—how much must his basic conception of the analyst influence the selection of what he brings? And how much are we not affected by this and by our own countertransference in what we are able to say? I am aware that the patient's free associations and our own analyses are intended to counteract this. But why is it, in spite of our analyses and constant self-scrutiny, that we can only conceptualize a patient's analysis to our satisfaction after it has ended? And why is it that the patient often does his most significant piece of analytic work, or even only tackles his main problem, after the analysis has ended?

In other words, what sort of secret loving and secret hating have patient and analyst needed to make the relationship viable? The loving and understanding situation of analysis to some extent rests on a social contract. One thing is certain; no patient tells or can tell his analyst everything, even of what consciously occurs to him. Every patient keeps his secrets, whether from a desire to keep an area of his life unanalyzed, to convince himself of his own power to contain his deepest fears, or because he fears to hurt the analyst excessively. But whatever his motive, it implies a considerable area of reserve. And however understanding and successful with a patient an analyst may be, I believe that most analysts begin to feel a definite sense of irritation if the patient dares to delay more than twenty seconds on his way to the door. And is it only because we work so hard that we all take such long holidays? All this must operate significantly at some level in the decision to end treatment, and even more in those treatments that come to an end because patient and analyst have somehow ceased to do constructive work together.

But all this gives a very one-sided picture of psychoanalysis. The unanalyzed transference may be an important vehicle of cure or failure of cure in analysis as it is in other therapies, but the specific contribution of psychoanalysis clearly lies in its interpretations.

Are we to believe that interpretations are simply the bus onto which the analytic patient's transference climbs just as once it climbed onto galvanic stimulation and perhaps climbs now onto deconditioning? Strachey was fully aware of this problem. He refers to the difficulty of knowing the effect of any interpretation because of the patient's libidinization of it. From time to time it almost looks as though interpretation were simply a bus. As already indicated, the analyst can experience and even show obvious intellectual confusion and the patient go from strength to strength. I believe that it is a mistake, though it is often made, to take the patient's progress as proof that the analyst must have "understood" the patient. But there are great difficulties in analytic reporting, and in any event such cases, though not uncommon, are not typical. The typical situation is as Strachey describes it, that there is a definite correlation between the specificity and detail of interpretation and the patient's progress. I would however add two riders. First, successful interpretation brings patient and analyst together emotionally; and secondly, as various French analysts have stressed, this presupposes the requisite moral qualities in the analyst.

Interpretation thus takes place in the context of a relationship, and we therefore have to be cautious in determining its effects. How much is determined by the content of the interpretations, how much by the subtle understanding of an unconsciously agreed code, how much by the authority lent to the analyst by his conviction? How does an analyst who is unconvinced by, say, Kleinian reconstructions of early infancy and the validity of the technique based on them explain satisfactory Kleinian results? As an illusion?—this has its danger for all of us: our opponents have always thought psychoanalytic results to be an illusion. As a partial illusion?—then on what did the results depend if not on interpretations based on Kleinian hypotheses about pathology? Simply on unanalyzed transference? Or on those portions of the interpretative work which were classically Freudian, yielding partial results in proportion to their classical acceptability? I do not think that many psychoanalysts would consider the hypothesis of such a direct relationship between the content of interpretation and the results achieved a convincing one.

Should successful results be explained by the cathexis by the patient of the analytic function, just as the child may cathect the functions of the mother rather than the mother herself, and so be better enabled to withstand some of the vicissitudes of changing object relationships? This would place the content of analytic interpretation as suggestion, its effectiveness depending in reality on the patient's affinity for the analytic method and to some extent the personality and interpretative slant of the analyst, perhaps reinforced in proportion to the degree of inner consistency of the interpretations. Or would such a sceptical analyst explain Kleinian results as being based on psychological truth, even though this truth is expressed in a symbolic language which itself does not stand up to logical examination? This would place Kleinian interpretation in the realm of religious truth and might raise doubts about the objective truth of all psychoanalytic interpretation. I believe that to some extent such uncertainties are inevitable in any historical type of understanding, especially when the basic postulates of psychoanalysis are scarcely subject to direct observational verification or even to much verification of historical evidence. This is a problem of many sciences in which, as Woodger has pointed out, controversy has usually proved to have been unreal or, in a recent formulation by J. O. Wisdom (1969), concerned not with fact but with *Weltanschauung*. What our controversies seem to show, however, is that with the lack of objective methods of assessment of the psychoanalytic process, our faith in our interpretative systems does not seem to show a high capacity for modification. "Confirmation" by the increasing comprehensibility of the patient's communications, reinforced by memories, and by the development of neurotic attitudes in relation to the psychoanalyst, often appear less impressive when scrutinized logically than they do in the consulting room. These "confirmatory" experiences are claimed by psychoanalysts who maintain that their approaches are incompatible with one another. As Bernfeld said in 1932, we do not so much reconstruct the past as build a model of the personality, and psychoanalysis shares the same difficulties as other retrospective studies. I have suggested in a paper, "On the Use of Historical and Scientific Method in Psychoanalysis" (see appendix A), that this model may have a variable shape and that some unconscious accord has to be reached between patient and analyst for its acceptance.

I am not here denying the value of interpretation and construction, so carefully studied by such authors as Loewenstein (1957) and Kris (1956). The human mind is satisfied, and in some sense healed, by what it feels as truth. In the case of psychoanalysis, truth is expressed in a system of historical explanation. There may be better or worse historians, and there may be historical systems which satisfy some patients by their complexity and subtlety, and others by their simplicity or flexibility. But it is true of nearly all patients that some cogent system of historical explanation is necessary for their satisfaction, involvement, and cure, and that these are the resources without which the analyst would be lost.

The role of interpretation therefore remains as classically

described: the detailed understanding of the patient's neurosis as it evolves, especially of his compulsive reactions to the analyst, in a system of linked hypotheses, relating ultimately to the character given to the expression of the drives by early experiences.

I would like to return to the anxieties which interrupt this process of mutually satisfying interpretation and in the light of this to suggest some conclusions about the interrelationship of interpretation and mutual transference.

Strachey ends his paper by remarking that Mrs. Klein suggested to him that there must be a quite special internal difficulty for the analyst to overcome in making an interpretation. He points out that transference interpretations tend to be especially avoided and explains this by the analyst's knowledge that he will thereby attract a quantity of id energy upon himself. But he does not comment on the general internal difficulty in making interpretations.

In *Elements of Psycho-Analysis* (1963) Bion makes the point that interpretations are often made by the analyst in order to deny the anxiety aroused in him by the fact that the situation is unknown to him and correspondingly dangerous. This is obviously true of inexperienced analysts, but I would agree with him that it continues to operate. Bion's formulation is, however, a very general one, in which he equates the dangerous with the unknown. Here he might have taken a leaf out of Strachey's book, since the compulsion to interpret must clearly be related to anxiety over the analyst's relationship to the patient.*

How can this anxiety be defined? Partly as Strachey does, as the fear of the id impulses which will be directed at him. But if such a fear on the part of the analyst is to be

---

*Bion has, of course, returned to the problem of interpretation, for instance in *Attention and Interpretation* (1970).

comprehensible, we must look at it in more detail. It must relate to the analyst's anxiety over what he may be forced to experience and over how he may react as a consequence.

He may, for instance, react with aggression. Instead of empathizing with the patient, he may find himself irritated or bored by him, and begin to give detached or unsympathetic interpretations. It is a great burden to an analyst to have a patient with whom he does not sympathize, but it is not the analyst's tendency to aggression which is the fundamental cause of his anxiety. The analyst's aggression is after all his defense against a task required of him which he finds impossible. What he must be repudiating is his identification with the patient's primitive impulses which remain a danger to him—that is, the early aggressive sexuality which seeks to gratify itself by using the analyst as an object. If the analyst repudiates these impulses, it must be because of the danger that he too may yield to them. The analyst's underlying anxiety must therefore be concerned with the danger of introjecting the patient and, having introjected him, of responding to him at the level of the warded-off sexuality which underlies his character and values.

Interpretation must therefore serve to reduce the danger of excessive sexual stimulation for the analyst as well as for the patient. It is the analyst's ability to interpret which makes the situation tolerable for him and assures him that he will keep ego control. Perhaps this explains as well as anything why, as Bion suggests, the analyst may become prone to compulsive interpretation, or, one might add, to withdrawal. "Where id was, there shall ego be" is the aim of analysis for both parties, and interpretation represents par excellence the attempt to assert the role of the ego.

It now becomes possible to define more closely the mutual relationship of interpretation, transference and countertransference. Behind the patient's complaints, as Freud discovered, lies a disturbance in his capacity to love or to work, or, put another way, to integrate libido with aggression and with the demands of reality. The vehicle for the restoration of this capacity is the analytic process, and it acts in the first instance by encouraging the patient's surrender to the repressed. It does this in various ways: by abrogating reality by the use of the couch and of free association, by the analyst's confirmation of the psychic reality that the patient has warded off, and by interpretations designed precisely to awaken the warded-off impulses to further expression. The first quality of the analytic process in general, and of interpretation in particular, therefore, is that they excite sexual desire and, implicitly, by assuming the possibility of cure, which is equated in the unconscious with sexual liberation, promise to gratify it ultimately. Interpretation, therefore, itself becomes a sexual object, and the patient responds appropriately when he libidinizes it, as he invariably does.

However, analysis also contains a built-in disappointment. Interpretation is a substitute gratification. Instead of obtaining direct sexual gratification, the patient has to be satisfied with an intellectual formulation. Here interpretation has the role of limiting sexual desire, and it does so by pointing to the contrast between the patient's excited fantasies and the realistic possibilities. One begins to get a glimpse of an inherent struggle in psychoanalysis—almost a tease—which may partially account for the ambivalent relationship which not infrequently characterizes the attitude of the patient to his former analyst, and for the longing to return to analysis, which is often a more serious residue of treatment than is given due recognition.

What needs to be added, following Strachey, is that interpretation also sets limits to the analyst's counter-

transference. The analyst operates empathically by the con-
tro controlled use of projective identification. The more
sensitive he is therefore to the patient's instinctual impulses,
the more constant the danger of introjection, in order to
obtain the impulse life with which he has identified and to
counter the frustration aroused by the patient's inhibitions.

This predicament has great importance for understanding
the significance of interpretation as a regulator of psychic
tension between analyst and patient. During the working day
the analyst has little time for self-analysis; his energies are
concentrated on his patients. The first-aid interpretations
which he gives himself must therefore be couched in terms of
the patient's material. This is why he is liable to discharge his
own anxiety by means of interpretations overtly directed to
the patient. This is a second, more active way in which the
analyst operates by means of projective identification, and it
allows a tentative definition of one aspect of interpretation to
be made. In one respect interpretation is the technique of
agreeing to a verbal formula which will reduce psychic
tension between analyst and patient. The reduction of tension
tends to be an acute need for the patient; it is a chronic need
for the analyst who spends his life treating patients and
requires constant attention. I am not here describing the
special needs of a disturbed analyst. Analysts live by interpretation. It brings us emotional and intellectual resolution.
When we feel we understand something, we have to see our
way to communicating it. If we are deprived of this satisfaction it is not long before we feel restless.

Interpretation is therefore libidinized by the analyst as well
as by the patient, though in a way which is more structured in
the analyst by integration with ego and superego. It may be
this cathexis of interpretation with increasingly neutralized
libido by both patient and analyst which explains much of the

modus operandi of successful analysis. The cathexis of interpretation is the vehicle of displacement from the person. It is the stimulating sexual role played by interpretation which paves the way for the patient's introjection of the function of the analyst rather than his person and for the analyst to be more excited by his relationship with his work than by any individual patient. It may also be the cathexis of interpretation which is in part responsible for a lessened fear of primary-process thinking, and therefore for a greater potentiality for sublimation.

The decathexis of the person of the analyst is not an easy process for the patient, especially as his personality is given added weight by the whole authority of the psychoanalytic tradition. This authority forces the patient (in my opinion) to play, in some degree, a subjugated role. The proof of the degree to which he feels forced to accommodate himself to the analyst, and of his reservations about it, is revealed in the secret area which he maintains until after the analysis is over. It is often, or perhaps always, only after the end of formal treatment that the patient's repression-resistance is lifted in certain vital areas so that he can progress in a new way, using analysis only for himself.

For the analyst there is a similar but different problem. The psychoanalyst also sees the patient in a new way after the analysis is over, thus confirming the degree of mutual struggle which must have taken place during the treatment. Freud wisely wrote all his case histories only after the analyses were over. But the analyst who undergoes a training analysis has a difficult problem not shared by the ordinary patient, the effects of which deserve study. The trained analyst cannot forget the person of his analyst in the same way, or reestablish so easily the operation of normal spontaneous defenses. The identifications formed in his analysis are constantly in action, and he has to use perpetual self-analysis. I think that this imposes a special strain on him from which the patient is free.

REFERENCES

Balint, A., and Balint, M. (1939). On transference and counter-transference. *International Journal of Psycho-Analysis* 20:223-230.

Balint, M. (1968). *The Basic Fault :Therapeutic Aspects of Regression.* London: Tavistock.

Benassy, M., and Diatkine, R. (1964). On the ontogenesis of fantasy. *International Journal of Psycho-Analysis* 45:171-179.

Bernfeld, S. (1932). Der Begriff der "Deutung" in der Psycho-analyse. *Z. angew. Psychol.* 42:448-497.

Bion, W.R. (1963). *Elements of Psycho-Analysis.* New York: Basic Books.

——— (1970). *Attention and Interpretation.* London: Tavistock.

Bouvet, M. (1958). Technical variation and the concept of distance. *International Journal of Psycho-Analysis* 39:211-221.

Freud, S. (1913). On beginning the treatment. *Standard Edition* 12:121-124.

——— (1915). Observations on transference love. *Standard Edition* 12:157-173.

——— (1937). Constructions in analysis. *Standard Edition* 23:255-269.

Hartmann, H. (1964). *Essays on Ego Psychology.* New York: International Universities Press.

Heimann, P. (1950). On counter-transference. *International Journal of Psycho-Analysis* 31:81-84.

Jung, C.G. (1931). Problems of modern psychology. In *Collected Works.* London: Routledge and Kegan Paul, 1954.

Kris, E. (1956). Recovery of childhood memories in psychoanalysis. *Psychoanalytic Study of the Child* 11.

Loewenstein, R.M. (1957). Some thoughts on interpretation in the theory and practice of psychoanalysis. *Psychoanalytic Study of the Child* 12.

Nacht, S. (1962). The curative factors in psychoanalysis. *International Journal of Psycho-Analysis* 43:206-211.

———— (1964). Silence as an integrative factor. *International Journal of Psycho-Analysis* 45:299-303.

Racker, H. (1968). *Transference and Countertransference.* New York: International Universities Press.

Rycroft, C. (1956). The nature and function of the analyst's communication to the patient. *International Journal of Psycho-Analysis* 37:469-472.

Searles, H.F. (1965). *Collected Papers on Schizophrenia and Related Subjects.* London: Hogarth Press.

Strachey, J. (1934). The nature and the therapeutic action of psycho-analysis. *International Journal of Psycho-Analysis* 15:127-159; reprinted in 50 (1969): 275-292.

Winnicott, D.W. (1947). Hate in the countertransference. In *Collected Papers.* London: Tavistock, 1958.

Wisdom, J.O. (1969). Scientific theory: empirical content, ontology and *Weltanschauung. Proc. 14th International Congress of Philosophy.* Vienna: Herder.

3

Elements of the Psychoanalytic Relationship and Their Therapeutic Implications
(1976)

Confidence in the therapeutic success of the analytic method tempts analysts to overlook some of the strains it imposes on both patient and analyst. The development of transference is always traumatic for the patient, as is the longing for relationship with the analyst as a result of their intimacy. The development of psychoanalytic objectivity and distance, which have to be combined with ready empathy, are similarly an arduous task for the analyst. The period of depression which the analyst must endure before he acquires his skill is described, with its accompanying danger of the prolonged dependence of the psychoanalyst on his own training analyst.

*   *   *

The most neglected feature of the psychoanalytic relationship still seems to me to be that it is a relationship: a very peculiar relationship, but a definite one. Patient and analyst need one another. The patient comes to the analyst because of internal conflicts that prevent him from enjoying life, and he begins to use the analyst not only to resolve them, but increasingly as a receptacle for his pent-up feelings. But the analyst also needs the patient in order to crystallize and communicate his own thoughts, including some of his inmost thoughts on intimate human problems which can only grow organically in the context of this relationship. They cannot be shared and experienced in the same immediate way with a colleague, or even with a husband or wife. It is also in his relationship with his patients that the analyst refreshes his own analysis. It is from this mutual participation in analytic understanding that the patient derives the substantial part of his cure and the analyst his deepest confidence and satisfaction.

The evolution of the theory of technique might be thought of as a gradual victory, but only a partial victory, for the recognition of the relationship. This clearly had its reasons as it was liable to get out of hand in the early days when wild analysis was a danger, as it still does occasionally today. And the technique of interpreting unconcscious impulse aggravated resistance, resulting in the sort of sexual battle that Freud described in 1915 in his "Observations on Transference Love." In his last clinical paper (Freud 1937) he was struggling similarly with the problem of the negative transference, protesting that the hostility of a former pupil was nowhere to be seen at the time of his analysis. The path to an approach which is less threatened by the patient's feelings was opened gradually between 1928 and 1950 by Wilhelm Reich (1928, 1945), Anna Freud (1937), Melanie Klein (1948), with her concentration on the interplay of object relationship and character formation and the subtleties of the transference, by Winnicott (1947) and Paula Heimann (1950) with their utilization of the countertransference, and Hartmann (1950) who began to map an area of functioning outside the "seething cauldron" of the impulse life. All this supplemented the libido theory, which was too stiff on its own for an adequate description of the affective life, with a series of articulations which would make it more acceptable to the patient and ease the atmosphere of the consulting room. The way was open for an easier discussion of the actual relationship, exemplified by such contributors as Nacht (1957), with his stress on the analyst's "presence" and Greenson (1974), who regards the analyst's capacity for loving his patient as essential equipment for his job. However, there remains little description of what actually happens between patient and analyst except in transference/countertransference terms or any details of the strains imposed on the analyst by fulfilling his obligations.

The strength of the emotions generated in the psychoanalytical relationship is in fact played down. According to a personal communication by Willi Hoffer there was a time when many analysts wore white coats, no doubt to protect themselves. The ubiquity of acting out, to which Limentani (1966) drew attention, provides evidence that tensions which are temporarily unmasterable are regularly generated in the course of analysis. I have already made attempts to approach the problems of this relationship (see chapters 2 and 8). In 1972 I suggested that there was an element of a tease in psychoanalytic therapy since emotions are constantly aroused which the analyst will never satisfy. The patient has to be content with an interpretation instead, and I thought that the capacity to use analysis might be connected with the capacity to cathect the analyst's interpretations, which all patients libidinize, instead of his person. There seems to be little discussion of the possible long-term vicissitudes of the patient's longings and of the question of how far our techniques of analysis of the terminal transference, so far as we can judge them, actually stand up to the hopes that we place in them. It is strange, too, that there seems to be no discussion of the effects on the analyst of forming relationship after relationship of the deepest and most intimate kind with patient after patient, and the mourning which at some level must be involved for each one of them.

Clinical theory and the physical arrangements in the consulting room are designed to protect analyst and patient from these problems. On the whole they are very successful, but I think that the conduct of analysis could often be improved if certain neglected problems were recognized. I should therefore like to consider the nature of the analytical relationship in more detail.

The psychoanalytic relationship consists partly in the replacement of an object relationship by a mutual identification, or rather by identification supplemented by an attenuated ("aim-inhibited") object relationship. The nature of the identification is different, however, on the two sides.

The actual operation of these processes remains somewhat mysterious, but an attempt may be made to conceptualize them as follows. The patient withdraws his unsublimated instinctual energies from the analyst as a person, but cathects him increasingly with them as a fantasy object. His instinctual desires for the analyst of fantasy are reduced, or even neutralized, by interpretations elucidating the archaic origins of his fantasies. The extent to which the ego's functioning can remain autonomous against the massive stimulation of fantasy in the transference and retain a realistic picture of the analyst, and the means by which it does so, are not well clarified. This was clearly the area with which Freud was struggling in 1915 when he decided that the patient's love for the analyst was "genuine" and compared the dangers of the analyst's position with a seductive patient to that of the pastor who visited the dying insurance agent: the insurance agent was not converted but the pastor left the house insured. On the other hand, the patient's ego clearly makes an affective relationship with the analyst as a person and forms an identification with the therapeutically orientated aspects of the analyst's ego. This identification lasts him in favorable cases for the rest of his life, while the unsublimated aspects of the transference are analyzed away during the treatment. This theory implies that the distortion of the person of the analyst by fantasy has been too unrealistic to last and that the patient's passion for truth, his *amor intellectualis,* has been great enough to result in the formation of a powerful new analytic ego and ego ideal. The fact that the formation of an ego ideal normally depends on object loss suggests that this is also an area of theory in need of further clarification. Freud was never tired of repeating, however, that there were patients who were not amenable to this transformation; for them only the logic of soup and the argument of dumplings had any effect. One may legitimately wonder whether a great many patients do not fall into an intermediate class between these two extremes.

The analyst does not cathect the patient as a fantasy object in the same way. Occasionally he makes a transference to the patient, typically as a response to the patient's transference, but this is quickly brought under control by his own continuing state of spontaneous self analysis (Gitelson 1952). The analyst has to identify with his patient's mental and emotional processes in order to achieve empathy, but the identification involved in empathy is not enough. It is too transient and too uncontrolled. In order to achieve continued and deeper understanding, he must not only empathize with his patients but scrutinize their mental processes critically, continually testing the empathic identifications which he holds inside him with his intellect and with the affects which finally determine his judgment. That is, he must hold the patient inside himself cathected with just the right degree of ambivalence, absorbing some parts of the image into himself and holding others at a distance. Any object relationship which he forms with the patient will be on a highly sublimated level, any instinctual expression being subjected to considerable modification through the analyst's absorbing preoccupation with the patient as an inner object. The conditions under which he maintains this preoccupation are not the easiest. Into the isolated, physically immobile life of the analyst come a succession of intelligent, mostly personable younger people who bring with them the breath of many different lives. They share with him their deepest feelings, as well as feeding into him considerable instinctual stimulation by the stories they tell, by their appearance, their voices and their smell. On the whole, analysts manage this situation well, but considerable instinctual inhibition is involved. It is perhaps not surprising that their repressed object relationship occasionally overflows into massive identification, as when they embrace a patient's point of view (for instance of a marriage) or even—occasionally—introject his symptoms.

In order to attain and maintain this high achievement, however, measures have to be taken the drastic nature of which is overlooked. The usual psychoanalytic arrangement of chair and couch abrogates the characteristic cue for human responses. The infant at the breast fixes his eyes on his mother's eyes as he feeds, and the human adult makes love face to face, and not *more ferarum,* "in the manner of the animals." For the most intimate and prolonged exchange of secret thoughts that humans have devised the patient is prevented from seeing the analyst's face, while the analyst sees only the back of the patient's head or perhaps the rear side of his face. Sometimes he sits where he can see the patient's eyelids or sclera, thus (among his other reasons for it) allowing himself a small piece of reassurance of which the patient is deprived unless he turns round. The reciprocity of normal human response is also abrogated in other ways. The patient lies down, normally on his back, while the analyst sits. The analyst addresses the patient, or half addresses him; the patient addresses the analyst via the air. The intimacy of the relationship is being offset—perhaps as a necessary precaution—by a setup perpetuating the authoritarianism and perhaps the magical aura of the nineteenth-century hypnotist. It receives its theoretical justification in the rather Helmholtzian notion that, by turning away from the stimulus of the analyst's appearance, the patient is freed from the pull of reality and can produce the derivatives of his unconscious mental processes in less distorted form. There are practical experiences which correspond to this. The use of the couch does facilitate regression and free association in most neurotic patients. (I will give a more detailed explanation of the mechanism whereby it does so, later.)

It will be more convenient at this point, however, to draw attention to some possible effects of these arrangements on the analyst, in addition to the privacy of thought which they secure him. If the effect of turning away from the analyst is so momentous for the patient, what is the effect of turning away from the patient on the analyst? How does the analyst accommodate himself to being without the basic cue of human expression for ten hours a day, 200 days a year? Does it impose a strain on him? If so, what is its nature and what means are available for him to alleviate it? I will return to this

later. But first I would like to sketch out some aspects of the
analytical relationship in more detail. I hope it will not be
thought that I exaggerate the difficulties. If I do, I believe
that I err in the right direction because I think that they
require more open consideration than they receive.

I should like to start with a description of the position of the
newly qualified psychoanalyst. This description may not
apply with the same force to those who have practiced
psychotherapy for many years in a psychoanalytically orientated institution as to those who come fresh to more or less
full-time analytic work after being students. The newly
qualified analyst is confronted by quite severe object loss on
several fronts as well as by what might be called ego loss.
First, he probably loses his analyst, and this at a time when
analytical support might be very useful to him. Next, he loses
the object relations of his daily working life if he gives up his
previous career completely, or at any rate a good many of
them—the undervalued but important exchanges which do so
much to give us the sense of belonging to a community.
Above all, his instinctive desire to form object relationships
with his patients is frustrated, lying at the root, perhaps, of
much countertransference difficulty until he can accommodate himself to the psychoanalytic way of life. All this may be
obscured to some extent and for a time by the relief of
qualifying and the excitement of starting his longed-for
career. What will not be obscured is the sense of loss of an
ego: the intellectual task of following the evolution of unconscious themes in his patients' words and behavior, relating
them to an effective notation and considering them in such a
way as to be able to produce a spontaneous and more or less
effortless interpretation, is immensely difficult. When it is
achieved, it restores the sense of reality to the analyst's ego.
Many analysts admit, however, that it took them many years

to feel themselves to be analysts and to be able to accept most patients who were recommended, without experiencing some degree of anxiety and guilt. The analyst's professional role is thus for a long time alienated from his full sense of identity. In this plight he must cathect the inner representations of his teachers, first of his analyst, then of the idealized image of the great man or woman who represents authority to him. This feeling of therapeutic inadequacy might be called the depressive position of the newly qualified analyst. The great figures will have a tendency to operate in him as introjects, he will look for opportunities to apply their formulations rather than his own, and he may even find himself occasionally mouthing bad interpretations from the book twenty years later.

To sum up, it will be seen that I regard the beginning of psychoanalytic practice as involving, in addition to its satisfactions, a depressive experience as a result of object loss and separation between the ego and the ego ideal, against which the analyst tries to defend himself by introjection. Of course, he also defends himself by seeking new teachers in the external world and discussing cases with his colleagues in seminars. I do not think that he can entirely escape the effects of having to relate to patients as internal objects rather than external objects in this way, however. And while he clearly needs support and further education, there may come a danger point at which the search for his own originality and authority becomes submerged by further introjections. This way also lies the danger of idealization of ambivalently cathected leaders, which may overwhelm individual judgment.

If beginning the practice of analysis holds these strains for the analyst, what strains does beginning analysis hold for the patient? To my mind, though it may be heavily concealed by improvement, beginning analysis must be described as a trauma for the patient.

The essence of a traumatic situation, according to Freud, is "an experience of helplessness on the part of the ego in the face of accumulation of excitation whether of external or internal origin" (1926) and also "a breach in an otherwise efficacious barrier against stimuli" (1920). The barrier that is breached in analysis is, of course, the barrier against the excitation of unconscious fantasy and unconscious memory. The psychoanalytic arrangements are designed to effect this breach for therapeutic purposes. I should say at once that the arrangements and interpretation are also designed to contain the trauma and reduce it from the start. I believe, however, that our confidence in our therapeutic efficiency and the quickening of object relationship that characterizes the start of a new analysis induce in us a tendency to underrate the drastic nature of what we do.

The patient is asked to sacrifice the reassurance of his previous contact with the analyst, eye to eye, ego to ego. The reason why patients are often, or perhaps always, afraid to lie on the couch is that they understand one of its essential meanings. This is the loosening of the grip of their ego on reality at the very time when enormous intrapsychic demands are imposed on its synthetic function under the influence of a powerful new object relationship. The abrogation of response by the analyst is compounded by the withholding of a great many normal comments and answers to questions. The patient is thus, so to speak, dropped by the analyst from the point of view of the role that he exercised at the consultation as a member of the externally real, holding environment. The patient who has been "dropped" in this way has to clutch at a new object relationship, in the first instance hypercathecting the analyst's words. He is reassured by the genuine object cathexis which he feels from the analyst, but a split has occurred in his ego. The experience of being dropped from the analyst's holding environment to being held by the Word alone results in the analyst's being jet-propelled in the patient's mind into magical status. The patient's new, intensified object relationship with the analyst becomes steadily more invested with fantasy. Transference phenomena begin to occur. The realistic ego which operates with energies further removed than the fantasies from their instinctual sources and which makes a realistic relationship with the analyst is rendered less potent. It is confronted by strange, involuntary thoughts which it tends to repudiate. The patient has begun to enter the world of waking dreams. These dreams take over, or partially take over, in the consulting room, and sometimes outside it, for several years. What the development of the transference has shown is the power of analysis, aided by the couch/chair arrangement, to remobilize the past traumatic introjections which the patient can now no longer contain. He has to rely on a stranger to help him with his problems and, sensing their complexity, he may rightly apprehend that the stranger, whatever his capacity to respond, will fail to understand him adequately in some important areas with which he will have to struggle on his own after the analysis is over. His confidence in his power to continue his own analysis may have been diminished by an assault on the ego, of whose dangers Ernst Kris (1956) was well aware: the sudden release of repressed memories, to which might be added the effect of wonderful interpretations and sometimes of interpretations which speak too quickly of the patient's aggression rather than of the anxieties behind it. All this aggravates the trauma, and it seems justified to conclude from the recognized phenomenon of the honeymoon period, that the patient instinctively copes with it by employing manic defenses.

Of course, the therapeutic action of psychoanalysis starts immediately. In spite of his anxieties, the patient will usually feel enormously reassured by the analyst's ability to demonstrate his capacity to accept and understand his feelings in a way which is a totally new experience for him.

The problem is: to what extent can interpretation resolve the developing wishes directed at the amalgam of the analyst as a real and fantasy object? According to the classical theory only pregenital impulses could be sublimated, though this is now generally doubted. The nature of the capacity for sublimation is clearly relevant, however, to the question of what elements of the transference can reasonably be expected to be resolved. Freud recognized that there was a problem in this area when he referred to the fact that in some respects the patient's love was "genuine," that is, presumably that it included an element which could not simply be analyzed away. The question of how far analysis in fact leaves the patient to struggle with these residual feelings, in spite of our efforts to resolve them, is clearly important for the patient's development in the lifetime that should await him undisturbed after he has left the analyst's room for the last time. If he is left with unreciprocated love and unresolved hostility then this is a difficulty of the psychoanalytic procedure which must be examined.

The residual bond (to which the analyst always responds in some way) is most clearly seen in training analysis. Freud, still rather naive about transference matters, regarded the bond that springs up between the candidate and his analyst as "not least" of the gains of analysis. Perhaps we are now entitled to be more suspicious that a prolonged dependency of thought may also sometimes arise. Although a similar bond is less easy to observe in former patients who are not analysts, we may suspect that it remains strong in some of them—those patients, for instance, who, in spite of the gains of analysis, still lead unsatisfying lives, in some depressed patients, and patients whose lives have been dramatically changed by analysis. It has remained strong in those patients who, in spite of their ambivalence, return to the same analyst in an attempt to put things right between them, and in those patients who move over a period of twenty years from one analyst to another. Two other phenomena, or possible phenomena, may also give rise to thought. One is that it seems to be not uncommon for patients to harbor resentment against their former analysts. There must, of course, be many explanations for this, but the tease inherent in stimulating and frustrating emotions could be one of them. The second phenomenon, if it exists, is of a comparable kind on the part of the analyst. There sometimes seems to be almost a tendency among psychoanalysts, or at any rate a temptation, to sabotage their relationship with their patient after termination. If this impression has any truth in it, then it implies that the strain of countertransference feelings is also not easily dealt with. After all, how can we be expected to allow patients to impose so much instinctual restraint on us and not to resent them for it?

Whether it is true or not, it raises questions of the long-term effect of analytic work on the analyst which deserve consideration. The mourning of an analyst for his patients would not be directly comparable in kind to the residual mourning of his patients. Nonetheless, if it is true that the inhibition of object relationship with the patient imposes a strain, then it is likely to result in some form or degree of introjection to compensate for the gratifying object that has been lost. This may operate in manifold ways, but it could, for instance, be in part by the introjection of the uncivilized parts of particular patients with whom the analyst has to deal, resulting in an excessive tolerance of aggression in certain areas, with strong reaction formations against it in others. My own opinion is that such a process probably does affect many analysts early in their career, but they work through it with maturity. If this is true, it is very important to consider how the atmosphere of psychoanalytic training and the organization of a psychoanalytical society could foster it or diminish it.

*   *   *

The therapeutic implications of the views of the psychoanalytical relationship which I have presented center, as far as the patient is concerned, on the resolution of two problems: the trauma that he has undergone and the mourning that he may be left with. The two problems are related.

Whom does the patient mourn? Is it the analyst with whom his ego makes a relationship, or is it the analyst of fantasy who has attracted to himself previously unconscious impulses and longings? As in normal love and hate, it must always in some degree be both, since the analyst of reality could not mean so much to him unless he also represented the archaic figures with which we need to maintain a relationship throughout our lives. This is the crux of the matter. In the psychoanalyst the patient finds again the amalgam of fantasy and reality that he met in his first analyst of childhood—the mother who understood the thoughts he could not verbalize.

If the patient is to overcome his attachment to the analyst, more is required than simply interpretation of the transference fantasies because, put more accurately, it can only be a question of the interpretation of such transference fantasies as the patient is able, consciously or unconsciously, to make available to the analyst, and the analyst able to recognize and understand. The patient must therefore also reach a less intense relationship with the person of the analyst which has been bathed and interpenetrated by the transference fantasies by a route which allows his ego opportunity to assess the analyst's real attributes.

This underlines that the first requirements of analytic technique must therefore be to facilitate the patient's capacity to communicate his feelings and thoughts as fully as possible. In order to do this, it is of the greatest importance that the analyst should not reinforce the trauma the patient has experienced by behaving in an unnecessarily traumatic way himself. In order to reduce the split between the analyst of fantasy and the analyst apprehended in detail by the ego, a constant aim must be to facilitate the integration of the two images by the interpretation of the patient's warded-off perceptions of reality and, sometimes, in my opinion, by the acknowledgment of their accuracy by the analyst.

Much of this may be considered to be the common ground of all analysts, but I believe that in fact pinpointing the problems of trauma and mourning leads to a subtly different attitude and technique. For instance, analysts will be less inclined toward the traumatic use of silence, which drives the patient into silence or into concealing his feelings of rejection and his depression. The use of prolonged silence has already been criticized on these grounds by the Kleinian school. But although we know too little of what our colleagues really do, it seems to me that analysts are often oversensitive in their fear of disturbing the transference. If they become more aware of the traumatic factors involved, they may examine their techniques and be surprised to discover unnecessary areas of traumatization or failure to detraumatize. Do we sometimes pay too high a price for the sophistication of our techniques, for instance, if we reply only with an interpretation? To take another example: some analysts do not reply to Christmas cards. They analyze the patient's motives for

sending one when he returns. Is it really sound to imagine that
more is to be gained by rebuffing the patient in this way than
by reciprocating as a member of society with a common
culture and still analyzing the motives when they come up? Is
it really sound to act as though the patient had no knowledge
of one's private life and family, or even of the severe blows
that fate may deal one? It seems to me important that the
patient should be relieved so far as possible (it is a delicate
area) of the oppressive feeling, which he does not necessarily
express, that the analyst has adopted a Jehovoid stance, able
to control completely the irruption into the consulting room
of human joy or sorrow. Of course there are dangers in this
procedure in comparison with the classical idea of the analyst's prime function as remaining, so far as possible, simply a
mirror; but these disadvantages have to be weighed against
the disadvantages of the patient's suppressing responses
through negative attitudes to the analyst's rejection, which
may then become difficult to elicit.

The gradual acknowledgment of reality increases the sense
of reciprocity with his patient for the analyst too. He feels
more real: the split between his professional personality and
his real personality is reduced. I am not here suggesting—and
I hope I will not be misunderstood—that he should step out of
his role or have any object relationship with his patient which
is not confined, and remains confined, within the framework
of analysis and termination. The sort of relationship I am
describing does not interfere with the development of a
hostile transference, though this would clearly be its danger if
abused. But it does, I believe, help to prevent the suppression
of a secret hostile relationship and transference, and of
defensive idealization.

The maintenance of a relationship between patient and
analyst that is a hint, and only a hint more reciprocal than is

envisaged in the usual model also protects the analyst against the dangers of introjecting a fantasied ideal of psychoanalysis which may impose on him an illusory standard of normality. This may affect his treatment of patients deleteriously and even disturb his emotional balance for many years. Man does not live by reality alone, even less by psychic reality. It is good for analyst and patient to have to admit some of the analyst's weaknesses as they are revealed in the interchange in the consulting room. The admission of deficiencies may help patient and analyst to let go of one another more easily when they have had enough. In other words, the somewhat freer admission of realities—but not too free—facilitates the process of mourning which enables an analysis to end satisfactorily. The end of analysis is in this way prepared from the beginning.

REFERENCES

Freud, A. (1937). *The Ego and the Mechanisms of Defence.* London: Hogarth.

Freud, S. (1915). Observations on transference love. *Standard Edition* 12:157-173.

—— (1920). Beyond the pleasure principle. *Standard Edition* 18:1-64.

—— (1926). Inhibitions, symptoms and anxiety. *Standard Edition* 20:77-175.

—— (1937). Analysis terminable and interminable. *Standard Edition* 23:209-253.

Gitelson, M. (1952). The emotional position of the analyst in the psychoanalytic situation. *International Journal of Psycho-Analysis* 33:1-10.

Greenson, R. (1974). Loving, hating and indifference towards the patient. *International Review of Psycho-Analysis* 1:259-266.

Hartmann, H. (1950). Comments on the psychoanalytic theory of the ego. In *Essays on Ego Psychology*. New York: International Universities Press, 1964.

Heimann, P. (1950). On counter-transference. *International Journal of Psycho-Analysis* 31:81-84.

Jones, E. (1957). *The Life and Work of Sigmund Freud*. Vol. 3. London: Hogarth.

Klein, M. (1948). *Contributions to Psycho-Analysis, 1921-1945*. London: Hogarth.

Kris, E. (1956). The recovery of childhood memories in psychoanalysis. *Psychoananalytic Study of the Child* 11.

Limentani, A. (1966). A re-evaluation of acting out in relation to working through. *International Journal of Psycho-Analysis* 47:274-282.

Nacht, S. (1957). Technical remarks on the handling of the transference neurosis. *International Journal of Psycho-Analysis* 38:196-203.

Reich, W. (1928). On character analysis. In *The Psychoanalytic Reader*, ed. R. Fliess. London: Hogarth, 1950.

——— (1945). Character Analysis. 2nd ed. New York: Orgone Institute Press.

Winnicott, D.W. (1947). Hate in the countertransference. In *Collected Papers*. London: Tavistock, 1958.

4

Analyses That Cannot
Be Terminated
(1977)

I had already emphasized that the patient's longings for the
analyst are not easily resolved, and persist after termination.
In this paper I described the problem of patients who cannot
give up analysis. I concluded that not many analyses are in
fact interminable, as the patient almost always wishes eventually to stand on his (or perhaps more often her) own feet.
An etiological factor in lengthy analyses is early maternal
deprivation. I describe two cases in which this had been
compensated by bondage to a sibling, and this bondage was
repeated in the transference. The inability to relinquish
analysis was due to the resulting inability to internalize the
analyst except as an internal figure demanding obedience.
The patients feared that if they left they would be saddled

with an introjection on the pattern of their bondage. If termination is imposed by the analyst it is unreal—such patients move to a second analyst. The analyst therefore has to see it through. The cases that do prove to be more or less interminable seem to be truly borderline patients, not merely patients with a difficulty in engaging with current reality as a result of unresolved grieving. An additional barrier to termination is the seductive quality of borderline patients whose primitive sexuality is near the surface.

*　*　*

Analyses which are truly interminable are probably fairly rare. What I would like to discuss are cases still beset with difficulty after many years, which neither patient nor analyst feels able to end. However, it is the difficulty of these cases, not the length of time, which accounts for their sometimes being thought of as interminable. As Nunberg (1954) pointed out in his paper on the evaluation of results, some analyses in which a reasonable resolution is nonetheless to be looked for can be expected to take a very long time.

I am going to sketch out some aspects of the history and summarize some of the common features and differences in two lengthy cases, both of women, who are still with me in what is now modified analysis. I think of the first of them only as slow with difficulties in termination. But it is just for this reason that it may be helpful to describe her, as slow analysis and interminable analysis may have something in common, and the factors which act to modify the features of her pathology which are similar to those of the other patient will become apparent. I am aware that a comparison of only two patients is inadequate for the formulation of a scientific hypothesis, but I hope that it will be a stimulus to further thinking about a problem that deserves more discussion than it receives. I will end with some comments on the part played by the analyst in rendering an analysis interminable, with particular regard to the effects on his responses of the specific factors which characterize the transference of these patients.

It may aid clarity if I state my tentative thesis now. The pathology of these two patients had its roots in early maternal deprivation. The anxiety of their relationship to their mothers was mitigated by the transference of their dependency to a libidinally more satisfying sibling, resulting in psychological bondage to the sibling. The inability to come to terms with the loss of the primary love object resulted, as in melancholia, in massive ambivalent introjection of the love object. This introject was condensed with others, such as that of the sibling, and reinforced by powerful sexual stimulation, augmenting envy and sadism, and thus impeding the synthesis of aggression and libido. The difficulty of analysis is that the dependent bond is transferred to the analyst, and the patient fears a further introjection if it is terminated. The degree of resolution which can be achieved depends on the ability of the analysis to bring together the libidinal and aggressive components of the relationship. This is itself greatly affected by the degree to which the patient's ego is invaded by primary-process thinking.

Both my patients have been married, but their marriages have failed. I am going to call the first of them Mrs. N, for Not Interminable, and the second Mrs. P, Perhaps Interminable. Mrs. N was in five-times-weekly analysis for seven and a half years. The analysis was successful by internal and external criteria, transforming her capacity for work and love, and to a smaller extent for the admission of love. She then gave up analysis for six years. She returned for anxieties connected with her work and came three times weekly for a couple of

months. After an interval of a year she rturned five years ago
for once-weekly therapy because she still had social difficulties with men, was becoming socially isolated, and had a
fluctuating but chronic depression. She is now preparing to
terminate again. The later therapy has been moderately
successful on several fronts, with the emergence of new
material.

Mrs. P was in analysis five times weekly for five and a half
years. In spite of having worked through a significnt amount
of her dependency on her husband and mourning for him I felt
stuck and suggested that she consult a colleague. This she did,
but was not willing to transfer. My colleague described her as
one of the weirdest people she had ever seen, unable to talk
about herself as herself and relating only to part-objects. A
year later she decided to come only three times a week, then
twice. The analysis has had some success in that she feels both
less ill and more ill, and has achieved a greater capacity to
work toward artistic sublimations and to make relationships
with increasingly healthy men, but the effects of interpretation in the short term are often difficult to follow, as I shall
describe later in more detail.

Mrs. N-the first patient-had at no time in her life fitted in
very well with her environment, but she broke down on
marriage, which was a very brief episode. She went to a
psychotherapist for two and a half years, after which he
concurred with her view that she needed psychoanalysis. He
recommended an analyst, but Mrs. N took objection to him
and was very pleased with herself that she came to me on the
basis of her own inquiries. She was preoccupied with a fixed
idea that a distortion of her ribcage as a result of a congenital
disease, which was only noticeable with difficulty even after
it had been pointed out, rendered her disgusting to men. She
was also "an effigy"—the effigy on a fifty-centimes piece she

had given to her brother as a child so that he could have a whole franc. This memory screened her sacrifice to him of her early childhood domination with a reversal of their previous roles. The introject of the lifeless effigy was condensed with the image of her father, who had been dominated by her mother and whom she saw as a statue in a niche gazing unseeing over the crowd and about to fall. This lifeless quality of her own personality went back very early. In spite of evidence of relative maternal rejection and neglect, she had always been a "good" baby who never cried. She now acted the sightless effigy—which was also her father's penis, originally arresting and powerful but now destroyed—with men and with me, sometimes arousing something like fury, certainly in me, and I believe in them. Though her breakdown on marriage was linked with sexual anxieties, she has been able for some years to have normal sexual satisfaction. A feature of her sexual life, however, is that she has fantasies of having intercourse with animals.

Mrs. P was referred to me ostensibly for a flying phobia. This in fact meant an inability to fly with her husband and almost certainly the unconscious appreciation that he would be leaving her while her bondage to him would remain unbroken. It emerged in the analysis that Mrs. P considered that her psychological problems were due to a specific trauma in early childhood. She had been ruined psychologically when doctors appeared unexpectedly in her bedroom at the age of four and "removed a blood clot from her throat" after a tonsillectomy. It was clear that this picture represented to her a betrayal by her main parental love objects—mother, nanny, father, and doctor. She transferred her dependency to an older sister. She married on her sister's instructions and entered analysis on her sister's instructions. This sister has herself now been in analysis for twenty years, having been referred originally for kleptomania, which was followed in her analysis by mucous colitis.

I would now like to begin to draw some of the common strands together. Both these patients suffered significant early maternal deprivation. Both transferred their early traumatized dependence to a sibling with whom they entered a relationship of bondage. Both introjected their early objects massively and ambivalently. Mrs. N was an effigy (though also a devil without orifices who screamed and screamed in the earlier phases of her treatment). Mrs. P was pleasant, humorous, and had available from the beginning an impressive amount of common sense and a genuine wish to be rendered capable of normal sexual satisfaction. But she could be terrifying. In fact her general practioner rang me up when she was already in the waiting room before her first consultation to warn me how hysterical she could be. Another common feature is therefore unintegrated aggression. There is also a common feature in their sexual life. Mrs. N shuns the practice of perversion, but has fantasies of intercourse with animals. Mrs. P's marriage had always been characterized by the practice of urinating on her husband's penis, and when very depressed after her husband had left her, she used to take her dog to bed and get him to lick her vulva. In both cases the sexual interest in animals was an indication of how inhuman they felt their libidinal objects to be and how unsublimated their own libido.

To schematize the common pathological elements further: as described by Freud (1916), these patients were unable to come to terms with object loss. They still sought their objects in the external and internal world, entering psychological bondage and introjecting massively. They discharged the aggression in their relationships largely by means of these distorted introjects. Both patients were subject to considerable sexual stimulation while their libido was still largely pregenital, and their egos functioned on an all-or-none basis, making it difficult for them to fuse aggression and libido and reinforcing the instinct-dominated character of the introjects.

This split between aggression and libido and between the good and bad objects has been described as typical of the borderline patient and well integrated with the literature in Masterson and Rinsley's paper (1975) on "The Borderline Syndrome." But I would not really characterize Mrs. N as borderline, though I would Mrs. P. And this brings me to the differences between them. Some of these differences, however, will be differences of variation only on a similar theme.

First, their manner of coming to analysis was different. Mrs. N suggested analysis for herself and had the conscious aim of reacquiring her own personality, especially her personality as a woman. Mrs. P came on the recommendation of her husband's psychotherapist and her sister, who had at that time been in analysis (with considerable improvement) for about eight years. She wished to overcome a flying phobia, but only partially connected this symptom with her increasing estrangement from her husband's way of life. On the other hand, she did link her analytic aim with one connected with her femininity: she, too, could not feel a proper woman while she was capable of orgasm only in cunnilingus and not in genital intercourse.

Next, while both patients showed evidence of psychotic processes, their manifestation was different. Mrs. N had a quasi-delusional symptom about her appearance, but her general character showed only rather extreme depressive self-devaluation. Her incorporative wishes and envy were largely contained in symptoms. There was little evidence of primary-process functioning in the transference relationship. Mrs. N's actual relationship with me was reasonably normal. Mrs. P's relations with me on the other hand were as volatile as they could be within the context of extreme dependency, and the sessions were characterized by bizarre magical think-ing, usually depending on Klang associations. I was constantly thought to be trying to control her thoughts—by movements for instance or by turning on the light. If I gave an interpreta-tion which, say, involved a reference to her sitting on the lawn, I would be giving it because the lawn is green and I wanted her to think about Mr. Greene. The screen memories which the two patients presented reveal the differences in depth of the psychotic process. Mrs. N's memory of giving fifty centimes to her brother is dramatic and with this reveals the strong role played by primitive defenses depending on the id, such as reversal, in its formation. But its symbolic quality was obvious to her, and its significance could be interpreted. On the other hand, the freshness of the affect in Mrs. P's story of the attack by the doctors and of the character change which followed it was in my estimation evidence of ego weakness and psychotic potential already present in child-hood. The residue of the extreme early traumatization which was implied could be seen in various ways: by her panicky need to telephone me simply in order to hear my voice, by the conviction from the start that I was lying to her, and her invariable conviction that any man with whom she had an affair was two-timing her (though this belief tended to fade when the affair was over).

This gives the main key, in my opinion, to the different attitude to analysis of the two patients, determining their differing potential for outcome. Mrs. P projects on to me the same kleptomania that her sister actually suffered from. In fact it is she who constantly steals my interpretations and hides them or conceals her thoughts by means of a flow of words from which it is difficult to extract the real feelings— what she describes as "never talking about the things I want to talk about"—in fact a sort of chronic colitis displaced to the mouth and to speech. It is her feelings of fury at exclusion and envy, displaced from a succession of childhood relationships, which prevent her from transforming my interpretations into a creative identification with an analytic ego and ego ideal and from allowing herself to possess me fully in the analytical relationship. The more she incorporates the good aspects of my personality, the less she can see herself as the exclusively good one, and the others as bad, and it is the destruction of this purified pleasure ego which exposes her to anxiety and confusion. It is this destruction that makes her feel both less ill and more ill. If she left me, she would be left with her confusion. She would have no chance of escaping it except by returning or by being possessed by the bad aspects of me. She could not experience my good aspects and stay away. She can only escape the intense anxiety and confusion of being a free agent by another confusion resulting from the introjection of a bad object. This mechanism is well in evidence when she uses Klang associations to undo the disturbing insights of the previous session. If she can localize her confusion by projecting it onto me and then reintroject me as a confused analyst, she can continue to function with common sense and clarity in her life.

Mrs. N, in contrast, can use analysis more easily. Her difficulty is the opposite one. She has to defend herself against an attempt to suppress her greed so extreme that she might incorporate my personality instead of her own unless I am continually present to give her permission in various ways to be herself—most importantly by listening to what she says instead of denying it and thus recognizing her. It was because nobody listened to her (responded to her feelings) in infancy and childhood that she had to scream so at me in the beginning. What she fears from termination is the reintrojection of a "lifeless" analyst who has no contact with her.

I should like to end with some comments on the difficulties for the analyst which arise specifically from treating patients dominated by such introjects. It is the unmodified character of the instinctual cathexis in their early object relationships which makes the introjects such rocklike structures. The analyst therefore receives a massive cathexis of unsublimated libido and aggression. I have maintained elsewhere (see chapters 2 and 3) that the difficulty in resolving the longings which analysis stimulates has been generally underrated. This is particularly true with deprived or borderline patients, whose desires can no longer be successfully mediated by the ego. The violent distortions which are the only means available to the ego for controlling impulse and the crudity of the affective and instinctual charges underneath the distortions make the material difficult to follow and to endure.

At the same time, at a deeper level, this massive stimulation with primitive sexuality and aggression makes the analyst wish to hang on to these patients since the patients' feelings evoke in him the desire to act in a similarly uncontrolled way toward them. He therefore wishes to keep them, and in his conflict over his desire for them as primitive libidinal objects, he introjects them. This leads to confusion and analytic paralysis which the analyst can only slowly resolve, and the patient scarcely at all.

A final word on termination. Does the rule which I nearly always follow—that the patient knows best when he has had enough analysis—apply in these cases? Or is the psychotic confusion too great for the patient to have a realistic judgment? I should like to state that I would always hesitate before imposing any other termination than one initiated by the patient. I believe, as I said at the beginning, that truly interminable cases are probably rare, if only because, in one way or another, the analyst has to free himself eventually from the strain and guilt of his confusion. But termination by the analyst can result in a trauma to the patient (and, I believe, also to the analyst) which at the time the patient conceals. Only the patient's decision to terminate can assure for him the preservation of the precarious identity he has acquired.

REFERENCES

Freud, S. (1916). On transience. *Standard Edition* 14.

Masterson, J.F., and Rinsley, D.B. (1975). The borderline syndrome: the role of the mother in the genesis and psychic structure of the borderline personality. *International Journal of Psycho-Analysis* 56:163-177.

Nunberg, H. (1954). Evaluation of the results of psychoanalytic treatment. *International Journal of Psycho-Analysis* 35:2-7.

II

Difficulties in Technique

5

The Structure of
the Session as a Guide
to Interpretation
(1961)

It is difficult for the young analyst to link theory with clinical practice. In this paper I tried primarily out of my own needs to apply Freud's metapsychological principles systematically to a session to give a guide to procedure. I suggested that the first thing to locate was the patient's anxiety, and next its expression in the transference. Anxiety motivates defense—what sort of defense is revealed? The analyst should ask only at the end what is the impulse against which the patient is defending himself.

In this way I encouraged the operation of the analyst's ego as a means of ordering the mass of free association to which he is exposed. I also concentrated on the condition of the patient's ego, which determines his attitude to treatment,

rather than on the fantasies that overwhelm him. This simple
paper proved surprisingly popular.

*   *   *

By drawing together some well-known principles of psychoanalytic theory and therapy, one finds it possible to
adumbrate a typical structure for the psychoanalytic session.
Once this structure is understood, it may be used as a guide to
the analysis of clinical problems. It is of course possible to
give structure to the session in many different ways. Probably
most psychoanalysts devise their own modes of reflection as
well as relying on intuition to decide their point of therapeutic approach. This paper aims to provide a conceptual framework which is relatively nonidiosyncratic, being based
straightforwardly on classical concepts.

Comparatively little has been written about the theory of
technique. One of the most important reasons must be that
both the analyst's mental processes and what he actually does
suffer so much distortion when he tries to set them down.
What I now say can therefore only be an approximation to a
description of my habitual method of working. I do not wish
to give the impression that it is my ideal to work like a
computer. On the contrary, I do not think that an analyst can
function successfully in an atmosphere of constant mental
self-discipline. When he feels, by whatever means, that he
understands something, he has to communicate it. I do not
think however that Freud's famous advice that the analyst's
attitude should be the counterpart of the patient's free association should be taken as a veto against the exercise of the
intellectual functions. I hope that my attitude will not be
misunderstood if I describe, as nearly as I can, something of
the procedure by which I usually guide my work.

I will begin by presenting a session as nearly as possible verbatim. It is taken from the analysis of a thirty-five-year-old aircraft designer of Middle Eastern origin, who presented with a strangling obsession. The analysis had lasted five and a half years. The patient was born of a self-made but drunken father of fifty and a mother of forty, ten years after his only brother. He had experienced an early separation of three months from his mother, being looked after by a married couple who were employed by the family; the husband in this couple later hanged himself. He had little contact with his father, but his mother was seductive at all levels. He well remembered a sufficient degree of lack of control of his bowels for his elder brother and others to make up derisive rhymes about him, but he was sure that his mother was never severe with him. As a small boy she used to help him urinate; that this had been highly stimulating was proved early in the analysis by the reconstruction of the scenes from the transference neurosis. The analysis of dreams had repeatedly yielded the somewhat puzzling fantasy that he was his mother's penis. At the same time, a feeling of pain in the back of his neck had gradually localized itself as a feeling of excitement above the left buttock where his mother had put one of her hands while holding his penis with the other. Her single male friend, whom she greatly respected, was called (in his native language) Mr. Fountain, so my patient in childhood had also been the Mr. Fountain that he fantasied his mother used as her penis for sexual purposes. This reconstruction was amply confirmed from other evidence. He had shared the bedroom of his prosperous parents until he was sixteen, observing not only the parental intercourse but also his father's drunkenness and violence. In early years, following their intercourse, he would often say "Mummy, I'm afraid," and his mother would take him into her bed.

Later in childhood it was his most moving experience when his mother would turn to him and complain of her plight in being married to his father. In adolescence he was once giving her a dutiful kiss when she popped her tongue into his mouth.

At the time of the session I had moved to a new consulting room outside my home following the birth of my first child. Some months before he had shown his first capacity to separate from me by accepting an assignment in France, having previously managed to avoid or refuse several similar invitations. For the first two and a half years of the analysis his sexual life had been confined to masturbation. Since then it had been reviving steadily. First he had compulsive inter-course with prostitutes, mostly in the open with some danger of discovery. This had been replaced by friendship with a prostitute. When this relationship showed signs of becoming dangerous, he began to visit models and masseuses. The masseuse to whom he refers in the session regretted the admixture of prostitution in her professional activities and was about to become his friend and cultural protegée. This was the path of gradual transition which led him to a Jewish girl—he was not Jewish—whom he met shortly after the end of his analysis and married about a year later.

THE STRUCTURE OF A SESSION

I had had a cancellation, and Mr. G was already in the waiting room when I arrived. He saw me come in, and I asked him to come with me to my room. His first remarks on lying on the couch were that his legs were hanging over the end of it as they had been on the couch of the masseuse whom he had visited on Saturday. This was a Tuesday. The masseuse had told him to move up on the couch otherwise his legs would be painful. He next said that when I had turned the light on as we entered the room he had thought somebody must have "popped off." He became rather silent, saying grumpily after a time that if I could find any value in this session, he couldn't. He then told me that a typist at the office—Mrs. L—had been sacked. He didn't know what the cause was: everybody at the office wanted to know. He had not complained about her; she was quite a good typist. But she had antagonized everybody, himself included. When he had been in France one of the directors had drawn the attention of a colleague to the fact that Mr. G had written a letter complaining that certain drawings had not been sent him. The colleague had been able to point out that the drawings had been handed to Mrs. L and that they had not arrived because she had not posted them. The director had said "If she doesn't do her job properly she must go," but this was many months ago. The idea came to him that perhaps she was being sacked because she was a Jewish woman. Actually, he then said, he didn't think she was Jewish. Then he said "Actually, it's an absurd idea." He said that when he had come back from France, he had brought a bottle of Chanel No. 5 for her, and her face had been wreathed in smiles and she had done her work pleasantly for weeks. Next he told me that when traveling to his session on the bus he had been thinking that he would do a shit here: he corrected himself, he meant in the lavatory. The idea had quite excited him—he had almost been gasping for breath. I interpreted that his frustration with the session was due to the fact that if he did his shit and produced his scent here his mother in the shape of myself would not be wreathed in smiles. I linked this with the session of the day before in which he had told me that he longed to be dried after a bath by a mother figure, such as a masseuse, but that if he were, he would dissolve completely into tears. I said the tears were the expression of his helplessness because if he let himself go, he would want to shit and would not be able to remain clean. He responded with two stories. His mother had told him that in his early childhood whenever she bathed him, he always promptly got himself dirty again; on one occasion she had found him in the flour box covered with it from head to foot. On a second occasion he had been dressed in a new sailor suit and had promptly got out and climbed all over the carriage wheels in the mud. Next he told me that he had brought with him his office towel, which stank. He always went on using his office towel until it stank and then gave it to his landlady to wash. She invariably commented on how it smelled, and he thought she got pleasure from the dirt too. She was always talking about whether the dog had done his duty and inquiring of one or other of the lodgers how much and how big, etc.

He then said that when he went to a masseuse he was very careful to urinate before she handled him, and this had puzzled him. Why, he asked me, did he do that? I said that it was to avoid his mother being brought too close, as she might be if he wished to urinate. It was a magical reassurance that his urinary and anal impulses towards her would not lead to a repetition of his infantile scenes with her.

The psychic phenomena of the psychoanalytic session are of a different order from those of the dream or even of symptoms. Instead of being purely or largely endopsychic, they take place within a close personal and professional relationship with a real individual. It is for this reason that the transference has come progressively to be regarded as the crucial phenomenon for study, since it is here that analysts can most easily see not only the manifestations of the unconscious drives but also their mode of integration with reality. However, the true elements of transference can only be accurately determined after the relationship has been examined on a realistic basis. It is first necessary to assess the degree to which the patient's attitudes may have been induced by the analyst's behavior—for instance, whether the patient's resistance has been provoked by the "omnipotent" or pompous behavior to which most analysts seem sometimes to be prone and which the patient rightly resents.

My first procedure is therefore to scan the patient's associations and behavior for any references which may be equated with comments on the situation between us. I examine everything that the patient says, first on the assumption that it also refers to his feelings about myself. That is to say, my first step in structuring the session is to try to determine the transference as it stands on that particular day. I am especially interested in anything which reminds me of the preceding session. The importance of the continuity of sessions was emphasized particularly by Wilhelm Reich, and later by Melanie Klein.

In this session the patient began by speaking about me overtly. He then began to talk of the excitements of his current day. A typist had been sacked, and one of the origins of the discontent with her lay in her not having sent him the mail that he needed when he was abroad. The attempt to link associations with the relationship with the analyst here became manifestly easy, and at once revealed a more defended series of thoughts. Did he mean that I ought to have written to him when he was in France? This would be consonant with his idea that one of my patients had "popped off,"—that is, from my knowledge of his fears, that he had committed suicide owing to my neglect. In that case I would certainly deserve the sack. The absurd idea that Mrs. L was Jewish would not be so absurd if he were confusing Mrs. L with myself. To Mrs. L he had brought scent. This had pleased her for weeks. To myself he had wished to bring the gift of feces and had come near to doing so in the shape of the smelly towel, destined after me for his landlady. This therefore would be what was required to keep those neglectful of their proper duties happy for weeks. (He had made similar criticisms of his landlady.) The transference in this session thus begins to be determined: he is compelled to keep going an anal relationship with a neglectful and hence dangerous analyst-mother who has failed in her duties. It will be remembered that this session took place shortly after the birth of my first child and that he had seen me come in. In reality I had taken the opportunity of the cancellation to nip up the road to my home and see how the baby was getting on. The first step in structuring the session—the determination of the day's transference—was beginning to be accomplished.

Since Anna Freud's systematization of the defenses in 1936, psychoanalysts have been accustomed in general to interpret defense before content. The usual motive for defense is the anxiety produced by an unconscious wish. My next attempt in structuring the session is therefore to ask myself the question, What is today's main anxiety? Whether the answer is to be found primarily in the patient's life situation or in the emotions aroused by the analysis, I again first look for its reflection in the transference. The most clearly expressed cause of his anxiety the day before had been his fear that if he were dried after a bath by a mother figure, he might dissolve into tears. The patient's whole analysis was dominated by the fear of expressing primitive grief to me, and therefore love, which would cause him to break down completely. This would not only have rendered him passive and helpless in relation to his seductive mother and therefore, insofar as he was an adult, stimulated his homosexuality—more important, he would have had to retract the hostility against her on which his health and sense of reality had to some extent depended, the strength of which was expressed in his strangling obsession. To avoid the unbearable pain of his conflict of love and hate and to reduce the anxiety evoked by the omnipotent fantasies accompanying them, he transformed his fantasies into sexual games. He would sometimes fart in the session for instance, thus proving that his primitive impulses were under control. Today he had expressed these fears in relation to myself. If he were to undo his actual relationship with his mother (and now with me) in which he had indulged her and tortured her by soiling himelf—the carriage wheels and the flour box—his sadness and mourning would over-whelm him. He had begun the session by expressing his anxieties over soiling in relation to myself. Would I tell him to move up and lie properly on the couch? That is to say, he was in conflict over whether I would help him to function according to the realities of adult emotional life or whether I would indulge him in his anality, in which case he would never have a mature relationship with me. The arrival of the baby had stimulated his fears of my withdrawal from him, and his jealousy reinforced the danger of regression to emo-tional and anal incontinence in the session—that is, to a time when as a baby himself, psyche and soma had existed as more of a unity. This was the basis of my first interpretation—his fear that, unlike his mother, I would not be wreathed in smiles if he produced his scent in my consulting room. He told me in a session about this time that his impulse on lying on the couch was to take his pants down and that that was his homosex-uality. But, he said, he had nearly said that it was his philosophy. One might conclude that in large measure he came to analysis to be freed from his philosophy of placating mother figures by a degraded sexuality. His deeper anxiety was, therefore, that I would neglect him in some way which would leave him with the hopelessness derived from the necessity of short-circuiting the unbearable complexity of his feelings of love, pity, and contempt for a mother whom he longed to rescue by genital love, but could only placate by means of primitive sexual discharges, and that he would, therefore, have no escape from his hopelessness but suicide.

The third element determining the structure of the session is the nature of the defenses stimulated by the anxiety. These emerge clearly in the final phase of the session and offer confirmation of the hypotheses advanced. Mr. G was careful to urinate before allowing a masseuse to handle his penis, and this puzzled him. The fear of urinating emerges in this ambitious patient as a crucial danger requiring a real act of avoidance. His defenses may therefore be seen as concentrated at this point. They could be defined as isolation, as undoing (the assurance that no scene of urination will take place, that is, that his sexual relationship with his mother would not be repeated), and, in the session itself, as regression to anal sadomasochism and passivity (his slightly teasing and seductive talk of shitting in my consulting room and his indirect reference to my neglect of my patients).

To recapitulate; the session has been structured so far by considering the following elements in order: transference, anxiety, and defense as they apply on the particular day in question. It remains to take the fourth step of determining the essential operative wish. This must be related to the point of maximal defense—and therefore be directed in this instance against a phallic activity. Stimulated by the birth of my baby, it proved to be the desire to rescue a degraded mother (prostitute, masseuse, Jewess) by means of love and adult sexuality. This is expressed in his assertion that he alone had enabled Mrs. L to do her work pleasantly for weeks when everyone else was against her, just as his sexual relationship with his mother had saved her when he was a child. His mother had also been exposed to a hostile environment as well as to her unsatisfactory marriage. The persistence of this wish will be seen when it is remembered that this patient was shortly to befriend the masseuse and subsequently to marry a Jewess. Its physical expression involved the danger of a regression to a urethral relationship, and these were the impulses which he isolated in reality with the masseuse and again in the session by bringing them at the end.

But this was a patient who had seen my wife and spoken to her on several occasions. He must therefore also have experienced his fantasies about his mother vividly in relation to her. Insofar as I represented his mother I must have been partly the substitute for my wife. As the neglectful analyst in my own right therefore I must also have represented his father whose sadomasochistic relationship with her he had consciously construed as neglect. He had begun the session with references to my neglect of my patients (he frequently also charged his father with neglect of him) and had followed it with an account of his own erotic relationship with a delinquent married woman (Mrs. L). At this level of the transference he was triumphing over his degraded father. "If I could find any value in this session," he had said, "he couldn't." In this way he destroyed my potency with his stream of urine and spent the rest of the session undoing his destruction by a pleasant cooperation. Here again then the operative instinctual wish is for phallic urethral potency. This wish was being expressed in a rescue fantasy in relation to his mother and as a triumph over his father.

This completes the description of my scheme for articulating the session insofar as it relates to the current situation between patient and analyst. However, every analyst is aware that if the current situation is approached with insufficient consideration of the whole history of the patient and movement of the analysis, he will miss the layer of experience which is essentially dynamic. The classical example is Freud's failure in the Dora case to analyse his patient's latent homosexuality. In trying to avoid such errors, analysts habitually review the patient's material in various ways, looking especially for omissions and contradictions. I should like to draw attention to one aspect of the help which may be forthcoming from a study of the structure of the psychoanalytic session.

Psychoneurotic symptoms are a condensed and exacerbated version of the conflicts latent in the character. When the patient forms a transference neurosis, he reproduces not only a second and smaller version of his symptoms. As a more profound phenomenon he demonstrates in neurotic form the character attitudes which lie behind them. By the time the transference neurosis is fully formed, each patient's sessions show a recognizable individual pattern. His character is manifest in his way of entering the room, in his relationship to his analyst, in his material and in his presentation of it. It could therefore be said that at the height of the transference neurosis each patient repeats in every session something of his whole life history. Such a proposition may strike one at first as extreme. I should like to make the experiment—in this respect truly at random—of examining the session just described in the light of this principle. I shall indicate my points briefly.

At the beginning of the session the patient was watchful of me but restrained in his manner. He had had need to watch his parents' words carefully and to be in some fear of their reactions. He started his communications by saying that he did not really fit the couch—he had not really been designed for his own bed either; he had been an "accident." "Someone must have popped off." Why had there been no more children? This was a reference to his childhood belief that his mother constantly aborted herself and to his parents' remoteness and his feeling that they neglected him. In maintaining his posture, he demonstrates his revolt against his home environment and his sexualization of discomfort, dirt, and depression. In withholding the weekend material until Tuesday, he repeats the reactive form of his anal eroticism. The whole incident with the masseuse refers to his need for an anal relationship with a degraded object and his discomfort in the relationship. After he recounted it, his grumpy remarks—if I could see any use in the session, he couldn't—express his dissatisfaction with the situation and sense of futility. From this he turns with excitement to his rescue fantasy about the typist, that is toward the idealized, inefficient mother who had antagonized everyone. Next come racial questions, which were important in the transference, since they had been of the highest significance during his upbringing in the country of racial and national conflicts in which his parents had lived. After the exalted thoughts of rescue of a persecuted mother he again turns to the somewhat despairing, jocular libidinization of drab anality and to his need to soil repeatedly and revenge himself on the mother he loved—that is to the tragic defeat of his heroic impulses in the regression to anal-sadistic clowning. Finally he determines that the path of seduction which chained him to his mother in a degraded instead of an heroic relationship shall not be repeated.

Certainly the patient had repeated many of the developmental themes from his childhood, and the sequence of events in the session illuminates their relationship. When puzzled by my patients' material, I sometimes take notes of the sessions for days or weeks as nearly as I can verbatim and scan them for continuity of theme, both from session to session and within the session itself. I would not claim that such a method infallibly bestows comprehension. The point of the patient's maximal conflict is also the point of his maximum emotion and maximum defense. It is therefore in practice the point of the analyst's maximum contamination with his patient's emotion. It is at this point that the clarification of the material by a formal scheme can be particularly useful.

6

A Particular Form
of Transference in
Neurotic Depression
(1966)

The conflict between the Kleinian school of analysis, which had greatly influenced the British Psycho-Analytical Society before the war, and the Austrian analysts (and their followers), who had arrived in England in 1938, was fought out after the war. The largest number of British psychoanalysts tried to maintain an "independent" or "middle" position.

The central Kleinian thesis seemed to me at that time to be that the capacity for psychological maturity was determined by the infant's development, from the age of a few months, of concern for a love-object now recognized as a whole person and the recipient of its destructive rage. This, as I understood it, was the essence of the so-called depressive position. The key to a more thoroughgoing psychoanalytic therapy therefore lay, according to the Kleinians, in demonstrating these omnipotent aggressive fantasies in the transference in all their primitivity, and working through the pain of recognizing that they were experienced in relation to an analyst who was also loved.

There was also another important influence in psychoanalysis at the time. This was the so-called ego-psychology of the Viennese American School, especially of Heinz Hartmann. This school pointed to the importance of the conflict-free or autonomous areas of ego functioning. Its cool and detached atmosphere contrasted with the emphasis in the British Society on the seething cauldron of emotion which constantly displayed itself in the transference.

My paper was an attempt to find a personal orientation to the analysis of depression which would explore the experiences of the ego as they displayed themselves clinically, and incorporate some of the Kleinian insights without being committed to the Kleinian timetable of infantile life or the technical approach based on it. It was influenced by Kleinian thinking in its stress on the importance of conflict between internalized objects, and in the importance given to the projection of idealized and degraded partial images in the transference. But it also attempted to incorporate more fully into the psychology of the depressive illness phallic and later oedipal elements, as well as environmental influences (which often seemed to have little weight in Kleinian presentations of the time). It ends by describing how an unresolved depressive position may determine the end of analysis for the depressed patient, who may have to terminate in order to spare the analyst the full force of his reproaches.

*   *   *

If a psychoanalyst tried to imagine a patient who was never "depressed" in analysis, I think his heart would sink at the prospect of treating him. Not only, as Fenichel (1945) pointed out, is a depressive mood an expectable affect in neurosis; it is in part by virtue of this mood that patients become amenable to influence (Winnicott 1941). The serious difficulties with which patients present themselves, and the analytic process which challenges their narcissistic defenses, make it impossible, in my opinion, for anyone still undergoing the formal process of analysis to reach his optimum level of freedom from depression in this sense.

The term *depression* is also used, as has often been noted, to refer to a spectrum of psychopathological conditions and to describe an affective state which may be fully appropriate to reality. In spite of the looseness in the use of the term, a class of neurotic patients can be recognized who react acutely and chronically with a depressive mood and who present a childhood history characterized by feelings of isolation. They complain of a failure to derive satisfaction from life and, to some degree, from analysis, and they constantly assert their feelings of inadequacy or hopelessness. These are sometimes temporarily compensated by denial, leading to an overestimation of their personality and abilities. The type of depression which such patients show is often designated "neurotic" or "reactive." Though this type of depression is contrasted with the self-accusatory melancholic depressions in which drive defusion has taken place and the self is attacked by its ideal, a melancholic substratum seems to me always detectable. In this paper I shall attempt to isolate some elements of the depressive transference and transference neurosis from the other elements of the neurotic transference.

The elements I shall consider concern chiefly the relationship of various parts of the ego to one another, or rather the relations of the object representations within the ego to each other and to the ego ideal, or ideal self, and the way in which these images are projected in the transference. I shall also bring forward some postulates concerned with the nature of the original object relationships on which such an ego-structure is founded. Three typical stages of the transference will be described. These stages are not to be regarded as necessarily occurring in a rigid chronological order. In fact they interpenetrate one another, but I think that their schematic presentation is justified from the point of view of the time needed for the full development of the situations in the course of analysis.

What are the conditions under which a depressive transference is formed? Sometimes it is said that a patient can be forced into a depressed condition by interpretation of aggressive drives before the anxieties to which he is reacting with aggression have been adequately explored. I have no doubt that such a technique is injurious to the patient, who may become both more disturbed and cowed. It is not of these patients that I intend to speak. I hope instead to describe a series of phenomena which I believe can be recognized however careful the analyst may be to explore primarily the patient's anxieties and not to bypass the processes of mourning or to stir the patient's guilt by a premature interpretation of his unconscious aggression toward his love objects.

The patients I have in mind may or may not present with a liability to depressive mood as a leading symptom. To list some of the presentations: a woman complained of headaches and crying attacks and of being afraid of becoming difficult to live with at the menopause; a man came suffering from acute anxiety that he might strangle a woman; other patients have complained of inhibition or instability in their relation to work, or of some form of incapacity for sexual commitment.

What characterizes the history of these patients, however, is that they have experienced a prolonged sense of isolation in childhood and have been oppressed by the inability to communicate. As a result they oscillated between anger with their rejecting parents (whom nearly all children try to defend) and feelings of hopelessness, futility, and inadequacy. Their images of themselves and of their love objects are confused and uncertain. Much speculation has revolved around the acceptance of a family situation which they experienced as profoundly unsatisfactory. In my own patients I have been tempted to think of depression as a deficiency disease, not necessarily as Spitz describes it in his account of early anaclitic depressions (1946), though early oral frustration seems to be common. I have on the whole been impressed in these patients by a heavily traumatic family background: separations, infidelity of parents, drunken father and masochistic mother, and so on. But it would be rash to generalize prematurely on the difficult question of the relationship between intrapsychic and external factors in the childhood of depressed adults.

What has resulted from their childhood struggles is that three features characterize their object relationships. They are afraid of loving because they fear the pain of disappointment. Their anger with their disappointing early objects is transferred onto their present objects, who never satisfy. And thirdly, their self-doubt, based on the feeling that their objects disappointed them because they themselves were unlovable, results in idealization of their objects, with the inevitable result that once a relationship is formed they are again for this reason disappointed.

Their ruminations concerning the role and character of themselves and their objects have crystallized in a typical structure of the self. The patient's images of himself are split.

He has an ideal image, libidinal and omnipotent, and a degraded image felt as uncontrollably aggressive. Because of the distance between the degraded image of the self and the image of the ideal self, the patient suffers from a disturbance of work proportional to the distance. The reason for this, in terms of ego psychology, is that the function of work is to approximate the image of the self to its ideal, and if the distance is too great this is felt as impossible. This split in the self-images reflects a split in the object-images designed to solve the problem of the patient's intolerable ambivalence. His objects have been alternately idealized and degraded, so that the ambivalence is solved by condensing the image of the self with the degraded partial image of the object, while a remaining partial image of the object is idealized. The image of the ideal self is formed on the model of the idealized object.

To take an example, Mr. R presented with a fear that he would strangle a woman. He held a responsible research post in the aircraft industry. He had had a drunken and violent father, and almost his only admiring early memory of him was of accompanying him at the age of three while he supervised the contruction of a new house. His mother had been a masochistic woman who had had to hand her son over to the care of others at the age of three months while she underwent a fibromyomectomy. Indeed, she had at first diagnosed her pregnancy as "a growth." Subsequently she seduced her son sexually in a somewhat gross manner. Mr. R was highly valued by his firm but was impeded in his further progress by the fact that he had never been able to bring himself to take the necessary examination. He regarded himself as "a heap of shit," that is, as not really a human being, but a "growth." At the same time he stressed his undoubted abilities, which were of no use to him, he said, "unless I could be Galileo Galilei." In character he was forgiving and gentle, unable to free himself from a number of self-imposed restrictions. To summarize: masculine sexuality was bad; to be feminine was good. The libido was directed toward ideal object-representations in the ideal self (Galileo Galilei and the masochistic "good" woman). The aggression was directed toward self-representations (for instance, "the heap of shit" unable to qualify) and to those object-representations with which the self was identified (exemplified by the strangling obsession in which he identified himself with the aggressive father in the primal scene). Though the choice of his occupation pointed toward a healthy identification with a constructing father, masochistic ideal and degraded self-images combined to prevent the patient from achieving effective social or sexual status.

THE OPENING PHASE

The depressed patient typically begins treatment by making the situation outlined in the case of Mr. R manifest in the transference. He first brings his hopelessness and failure, sometimes, as has been said, by means of denial and of "omnipotence." His comments on his inadequacy strike the analyst as exaggerated. In this way he shows his degraded self-representations. At the same time he invites the analyst to take over the role of his ideal image by becoming his omnipotent savior. Some typical methods are by asking for advice, by presenting the analyst with an acute problem in reality, and, in women, most characteristically by silence. Since these attitudes reflect a genuine feeling of helplessness the analyst may sometimes find it difficult to resist completely the role cast for him. The difficulty of resisting the patient's appeal to extend help may bring the danger of a subtly collusive relationship. Clearly, if the motives for the patient's dependency on an idealized object are not analyzed, nothing will have been done to help him deal with the degraded image of himself with which he will be faced outside the analytic hour. If his major conflicts are bypassed he will become secretly discontented with the analysis, and his depression will become more entrenched. This situation may be obscured by the fact that the projections of his degraded images onto the analyst may scarcely be in evidence during the analytic hour but appear only in the form of acting out in relation apparently to other objects. Equally, as the patient's appeals are an attempt at seduction covering his underlying aggression, the analyst must also be aware at this stage of the danger that he may react with hostility, thus depriving the patient of his needed good object. It therefore seems essential that the analyst point out the ambivalence of the patient's subservience to him, a subservience designed to allay the fear that the analyst will release a latent aggression in the patient which will destroy such precariously held object relationships as he has.

However, all this may not occur immediately. Instead the patient may hypercathect his presenting symptoms, which act as a defense against his depression, and the typical situation of the opening phase may not manifest itself until these have been analyzed. Mr. R, for instance, assured me again and again, for the nine months or so that his strangling obsession lasted, that he would accept any other deficiencies of his personality gladly if only he could be freed from his terrible anxiety. In the event, when the obsession subsided, never to return in the six years of treatment which followed, or, so far as I know, in his apparently successful marriage undertaken a year or so after termination, the relief from his obsession was considered by him to be of no value: first, since he could never be sure it would not return; second, because, as he now maintained, the real problem was his intolerable feeling of the frustration of living—of "lingering," as he called it. Nonetheless, even while the hypercathexis of the symptoms continues, the patient is still at pains to lay marked stress on his inadequacy or wickedness. The alternation of this with statements of his fundamental normality or even exceptional capacity and goodness again indicates that he is presenting to the analyst partial representations of his objects and their condensation with his split images of himself.

The opportunity to interpret the patient's ambivalence frequently occurs early in the analysis. If the patient protests that he is not capable of making use of analysis (his ideal object), then the analyst can reply that it seems that analysis is inadequate for the patient, and link the interpretation with the anger which the patient is suppressing in relation to his parents and others. Thus the analyst may interpret aggression quite early, provided that it is clearly in the context of the patient's positive relationships. If it is not, it arouses intolerable anxiety and can only be met by denial. As a result, the mourning processes are bypassed, and the patient's feelings of guilt and degradation are increased. To give an illustration, I interpreted a patient's withdrawal from her mother in latency in order to pursue her own activities as the consequence of her jealousy of her mother's closer relationship with her brother. In the transference I related her reluctance to come to analysis to her jealousy of my relationship with my wife. During this time the analysis seemed at a standstill. The patient's aggression against a mother whom she pitied and a brother whom she loved could not profitably be accepted by her. When, however, we could achieve the formulation that she was so pleased that her mother admired her ability to manage by herself that this enabled her to deal with her jealousy of her brother, she could immediately modify the interpretation by saying that she must, in fact, have been jealous of him, and informed me that one of the reasons for her withdrawal from me in analysis was that she expected me to admire her for it in the same way. She could then gradually bring her hatred of her mother for babying her and link it with her resentment of the analytic process as an indignity. In this way the patient may be made conscious of his aggression in an acceptable way. In practice, however, it is a difficult stage in the analysis, since it consistently hints at aggression against highly cathected love objects, and because it is sometimes difficult for the analyst to follow the patient's defenses closely while at the same time seeing so clearly the basic id impulses at work beneath them. It is then necessary to start by surprising the patient with examples of both poles of his ambivalence from small instances in the transference and in his less important relationships. The interpretation of ambivalence begins the work of integrating the degraded object-representations with the idealized object-representattions into a whole object, with consequent gain of reality sense. The analyst's emphasis on the patient's positive feelings helps him tolerate his aggression, since it enables him to see it in perspective and thus to evaluate his feelings of guilt more realistically.

It is a part of the depressive patient's relatively intact sense of reality that the relationship between the real characters of his objects, ultimately his parents, and his discriminating ambivalence is complex. This complexity is reflected in the patient's doubt and uncertainty as to whether he is justified in each specific instance both in loving and hating. In childhood the real character of the parents was a puzzle to him. These considerations seem to indicate that the depressive patient struggles with a real problem of his early environment.

A difficult situation may make a child sharp-sighted, early

aware of the emotional problems of his parents. It is also likely, perhaps inevitable, that the child will react with anger, followed by projection. The impossibility of forming satisfactory relationships would result in identifications with ambivalently cathected objects (introjections). This situation is also made manifest in the transference of the adult patient. Beneath the idealistic and ambivalent cathexis of the analyst based on projection, there is to be found an acute awareness of his real character difficulties. More will be said of this when the final phase of analysis is discussed. But it is particularly true of the depressed patient that before he will trust the analyst with insight into his problems it is necessary for him to assure himself by a number of tests that the analyst's understanding of the complexity of his feelings is sufficient to ensure a degree of communication which can lead him out of his childhood isolation.

THE MIDDLE PHASE

The interpretation of ambivalence—that is to say, of aggression in the context of longing—reawakens the patient's awareness of object loss. It is therefore in this phase that his frustrated longing emerges into the transference in its full primitivity, resulting in an oral regression not always easy to contain within the context of the transference neurosis. I will return to Mr. R, who began his analysis with a fear that he might strangle a woman. The first phase showed him his feelings of passivity in relation to the magical potency of his violent father. His father had had a helpful relationship with the patient's considerably older brother, eventually offering him a partnership in his business, and when he refused it, aiding his further education. By the time my patient had grown up his father had deteriorated too far to be able to foster a similar relationship with his second son, who regarded him with suspicious reserve. His strangling obsession dissolved in response to interpretations of his passivity, his admiration for his father's sadistic potency, and his guilt over his sexual relationship with his mother—that is to say, when it was interpreted as a defense against his passive regression in the face of oedipal guilt. It did not, however, disappear from the now established transference neurosis, in which the preoedipal core of the symptom developed fully. His relationship to me became dominated by an attitude tantamount to a refusal ever to leave analysis. The disappearance of his strangling obsession meant nothing, as I have indicated, as there was no guarantee it would not return. His refusal to admit that I did anything for him at all meant that he had me in his grip. He protested against every interruption of the analysis, leaving me each time with the feeling that I would be lucky to see him alive at the end of the holiday. A new obsession now replaced the strangling obsession in his symptomatology. On going to the lavatory, especially to public lavatories, he had to struggle with an almost overwhelming desire to lick any feces which might be in the toilet bowl. He came for analysis to my home at an evening hour and his desire to eat my feces became manifest. Not only did he desire to stay to dinner (the menu of which he could foretell with some accuracy), but my breath seemed to him to smell overwhelmingly of wine and garlic, as his father's had so often done. He wished to pay me fortnightly, in such a way that the payment would be for the week which had gone by and for the week to come. I interpreted that not paying me directly for what he had had would relieve him of the feeling that the cash he gave me (having counted it on the lavatory) smeared my hands with dangerous feces. That is to say, by paying for what he had not yet received (eaten), he wished to reassure himself that what he gave me was not destructive but was good money (cash). He thus hoped to deal with the fantasy denied by him—that the cash obligated me to him and put me in his power. He also made an attempt to deal with his aggression by projection, offering himself for castration at my hands. He proposed to give me a Christmas present of a beautiful little Chinese man carved in ivory. When I refused it and interpreted it as the offer of his penis, he began an orgy of compulsive sexual activity with low-grade prostitutes. Though the regression described was limited by his obsessional defenses it illustrates typical features in the development of the depressive transference neurosis. With the patient's realization both of his love for his lost objects and his rage, their idealization and degradation emerge with full force. At this stage the analyst is credited with inhuman virtues and vices. I had "a conscience like the Pope"—partly because I discounted too greatly the playful element in his sexual relationship with his aunt and his brother's wife; it would never occur to me not to declare the cash he gave me to the income tax authorities; marital infidelity would be inconceivable to me; I must be disgusted by anyone who went with prostitutes, etc. At the same time my greed, laziness, and inability to offer him anything but the "solution of a crossword puzzle" rendered his situation unendurable.

With patients in whom a serious depression dominates the clinical picture from the start the regression is likely to go further, and demands may become too primitive for the ego to mediate. Miss L was a senior business executive who was failing in her work following a period of intense grieving for a lover who had died. She developed early the symptom of being unable to leave my consulting room, and, some time later, would instead pour abuse on me for my inability to say anything conceivably designed to help her, though she only wanted a little sympathy. Such a denial of the analyst's situation in reality was already highly suggestive of psychosis. A considerable period followed in which she voiced typical paranoid delusions in a tentative form. One of the few signs that some perception of the reality of the analyst's character remained was demonstrated by the fact that she would periodically insist on giving me a check with which she paid in part for the extra time she had exacted from me. In this phase analytic work proved impossible. Her behavior was to some extent a reaction to a realistic anxiety. The lunchtime analytic hour we had agreed upon reduced the much-needed time available for her work. It was necessary eventually to recognize the impossibility of her ego's mediating her demands—and that the analyst could be capable of making an unsuitable arrangement—and I gave her a time which would both enable her to come late (as she always did) and to have extra time at the end. Miss L's attitude then began to change. She brought her sympathy for the birds she watched in her garden, and, through this medium, for her outcast father, who had attempted suicide and died in a mental hospital despised by herself and the rest of his family. It was not too long before she was able to cry for him in sympathy, and in a sense to forgive him his fantasied and also in part real sexual assaults on her by dreaming of the former head of her department (an idealized figure) next to a toad. She associated the toad with the subsequent head, who had sanctioned her compulsory retirement, and groped for some lines of Shakespeare:

> . . . the toad, ugly and venomous,
> Wears yet a precious jewel in his head.

In this way she brought together the images of the idealized and the degraded father.

It may seem contradictory that a modification of standard technique should be advocated after previously emphasizing the danger of being seduced by the depressive patient's dependency. But such an acceptance of her need at this phase of the analysis enabled guilt and aggression which had been mobilized to be recognized instead of projected: first, it reduced the disruption due to the burden of her realistic anxiety; second, it showed that I did not consider myself infallible, but was prepared to listen to her in spite of her abuse. All this paved the way for the interpretation of her fantasy that she had killed her father by her unawareness of his need. In my opinion a technique which recognizes the urgency of the patient's psychic and realistic predicament is to be distinguished from a technique of encouragement at the beginning of analysis. The latter impedes the isolation of the patient's real conflicts.

But when the possibility of analysis does not have to be facilitated in this way, and when the patient's confusion of identity has been sufficiently reduced by his understanding of his introjective and projective defenses, the most effective interpretation of the oral aggression has seemed to me to be at a point where it is expressed as a fantasy relating to adult ambitions. This may be not so much on an oral as an orophallic level. Mr. R had brought his phallic greed in oral as well as anal terms. In his childhood he had always awaited the experience of "marzipan," a wonderful substance which, when he tasted it, he found to be only marzipan. Marzipan represented both his father's fecal penis and the breast he fantasied he had been deprived of from birth. He restored this breast to himself by a fantasy that he had incorporated his mother's breast, which he identified with his penis. He was able to masturbate with his penis flaccid and, though in no way schizophrenic, had swallowed his semen as though it were milk. The strangling obsession had its childhood precursor in an obsession about the removal of a wart from his mother's face. He had pestered her to get rid of the wart, which he identified with her nipple, by strangling it with a strand of a horse's tail. Mr. R also used to strangle his own penis with rubber bands. His acting out became more realistically orientated at each phase of interpretation. But it was not until his greed for his father's possessions and potency appeared in the emotions surrounding his father's failure to take him into partnership that the regressed elements in it gave place to a sharing of sublimations. His fantasies had crystallized at the phallic level, and following the interpretation of the disappointment he had experienced he told me that whenever I made a good interpretation he always thought, "What a partnership we would make!"

THE FINAL PHASE

The liberation of the aggression in the context of love results in a diminution of the distance between the self-images and the object-images. The object-images no longer appear so unattainable. This enables the patient to feel freer to evaluate the analyst's character. In particular he seeks out his weaknesses, and thus attempts to test the reality of his degraded self-images against the reality or otherwise of the omnipotent object-images. It is therefore necessary to the reality testing and cure of the depressed patient that this process should not be impeded. He needs to gain confidence in his reality testing and to be allowed to affirm such real weaknesses in the analyst's competence and personality as he has been able to observe. Only if he can see that the analyst is sincerely prepared to recognize them, and, if inescapably confronted, to admit them, can he gain the confidence necessary to tolerate the degraded parts of his own personality.

In the typical case the patient will bring this aggression directly, and will confront the analyst with many of his most painful difficulties. In my opinion it is an error to interpret such confrontations in terms of transference without first acknowledging the possibility of the reality. This may be exceedingly painful, and I believe that most analysts will have encountered such experiences.

While the patient brings some of the analyst's weaknesses openly, he brings others in disguise. It is essential that the analyst should be on the watch for hidden implications painful to himself in the patient's transference and should not hesitate to interpret them. This will, again, not merely be painful but to some extent impossible, and the analyst must also avoid the danger of masochistic confession. But insofar as he can achieve their recognition, courageous interpretation of the patient's secret thoughts is necessary if the patient is to leave the analyst with an adequate confidence that he can pursue his ambitions in spite of his deficiencies.

However, the patient must also have his reservations on what can be expressed, as is revealed in every subsequent analysis with a second analyst. Such reservation is a particularly acute problem in the analysis of depressed patients, with whom the inability to discharge anger against love objects plays such a crucial role in the etiology. Since such a situation also represents an analytic impasse it is not always possible for the analyst to bring his patient to relinquish analysis without an element of persuasion. This was the case with Mr. R. In the termination made spontaneously by the patient there may be an element in the recovery of a desire to spare himself and the analyst the pain of the bitter personal reproaches which might ensue if he continued. Perhaps every patient is able to make some reproaches against his analyst only after termination. It is important that the analyst's account of his work also include, so far as possible, what the patient thinks of it, and how this is to be evaluated. With the introduction of the theme of the patient's undischarged anger, alternative methods of giving structure to the evolution of the depressive transference are suggested. Such an evolution could, for instance, be described in terms of the full development of the oral aggressive and reparative fantasies. But the word *depressive* itself implies the subjection of the ego, or of the self-images to superior forces, and I have concentrated on these aspects since it is in them, it seems to me, that the depressive state itself is manifested.

REFERENCES

Fenichel, O. (1945). *The Psychoanalytic Theory of Neurosis*. New York: Norton.

Spitz, R. (1946). Anaclitic depression. *Psychoanalytic Study of the Child* 2:313-342.

Winnicott, D.W. (1941). On influencing and being influenced. In *The Child and the Outside World*. New York: Basic Books; London: Tavistock, 1957.

7

Formulating Interpretations
in Clinical Psychoanalysis
(1979)

This paper complements the description of the difficulties in "The Identity of the Psychoanalyst" (chapter 10) by describing the mode of operation of the analyst who has achieved a secure identity. It emphasizes the importance of spontaneity in addition to intellectual control. Spontaneity introduces an artistic element which enlarges the area in which preconscious communication between patient and analyst can take place. It is through this communication that the analyst understands the patient as an individual and the patient forms a freer relationship with the analyst. This is a central area for therapeutic change which has been neglected because it is the area which corresponds most closely with the ordinary methods by which people understand one another

and less with the revolutionary discoveries which characterize psychoanalysis.

*   *   *

We have long- and short-term aims in psychoanalysis. The
short-term aim is to relieve the anxieties and conflicts which
the patient keeps in the forefront of the analysis. The long-
term aim is to foster his development by means of a process,
started in the consulting room, which will help him in the
much longer period of his life after he has left the consulting
room for the last time. The interpretations which we direct at
the resolution of immediate anxieties must be consistent with
achieving the long-term developmental aims. In these the sort
of clearing-up process which can conveniently be called cure
is a very desirable but not an invariable stage.

The long-term aims are usually summed up in Freud's
phrase "Where id was, there ego shall be" and by special
reference to one aspect of this—the patient's power to
continue what is known as his self-analysis. Both these
concepts are somewhat elliptical. My understanding of the
first of them would be that the ego must acquire an increased
tolerance for crude impulse so that it can express it more
easily both in direct and indirect form, thus increasing the
number of satisfactions which can become available. This
alteration in the ego enlarges the analysand's capacity for
frequent and sometimes sustained analytical self-scrutiny. I
do not know how far beyond this the capacity for self-analysis
usually goes; I wonder, for instance, how many trained
psychoanalysts can analyze their own dreams in depth with
any regularity? Be that as it may, some internalization of the
analytic process, perhaps in a modified form, accompanied by
an increased capacity for instinctual satisfaction, provide
practical and logical criteria of analytical success.

Such an outcome implies that the patient has enjoyed the analytical process (which I will not here further try to define) and has formed a trusting enough relationship with his analyst to internalize him as a function, just as a child, according to Anna Freud, internalizes a mothering function with perhaps only a loose connection with the actual person of the mother. Of course the analytic process is mediated by the person of the analyst with its strengths and weaknesses, which may facilitate or disrupt the patient's ability to internalize the function, just as the mothering function is mediated by the personality of the mothering person. What this paper is concerned with is the way in which the formulation of interpretations can foster such an internalization of the analytic function and the way in which it can set up barriers against it.

Clearly a satisfactory internalization of the analytical process is made proportionately easier the less the patient's resentment of the way in which the analyst has actually conducted the analysis is allowed to fester. This is not quite the same as saying the more thoroughly the negative transference is analyzed. Though transference and countertransference play a vital part and can be used in a broad sense to explain all the phenomena, there is more to the resentment of lying on the couch, of analytical technique, and often of the analyst's interpretations than can, in my opinion, be adequately explained by these concepts, unless they are expanded to differentiate more fully what is personal from what is general in human nature and development. Whatever the origins of resentment, no experienced analyst can deny that elements of it not infrequently survive with more strength than we would like. Indeed, in a long analysis the negative feelings sometimes show themselves more fully as time goes on, occasionally almost seeming to submerge the years of positive feeling. Much of this is inherent in the natural limitations of analysis in taming human destructiveness and in the inherent human tendency to project it. What I am concerned with here is the marginal area in analytical technique in which the approach to interpretation may modify these tendencies.

Psychoanalysis has both traumatic and therapeutic elements. The clearest indication of its traumatic quality lies in the fact that it regularly induces a flight from reality. This is the most dramatic feature of analysis, and we describe it as the development of transference. It is due to the disruption of the stimulus barrier against the unconscious, and therefore accords well with Freud's definition of trauma (1926) in "Inhibitions, Symptoms and Anxiety" as an experience of helplessness of the ego in the face of accumulation of excitation whether of external or internal origin. I am sure that many psychoanalysts remember the experience of their ego being partially put out of action quite vividly from their own analysis. The traumatic power of analysis may be inferred from the patient's attempts to defend himself against the transference by projecting it into the outside world and trying to solve it there. A not infrequent example is by starting a sexual relationship at the beginning of analysis which may end as marriage as a defense against ending the analysis—that is, against the full power of the transference at all stages.

The sudden, traumatic development of transference creates a distance between the patient and the analyst. The patient feels that he is not his own master, while the analyst is elevated to a magical superiority. The essential craft of the psychoanalyst consists in undoing this distance by identifying the unconscious impulses that spill over to form the patient's image of him. The classical paper describing this process and its role at the center of technique is James Strachey's "The

Nature of the Therapeutic Action of Psycho-Analysis" in 1934. It represented a considerable advance in explaining the vital role of transference interpretation, but it left a number of difficulties. First of all, is it really true that only transference interpretations are "mutative" and that all others, or almost all others, are only a preparation? My own opinion is that it is not, though non-transference interpretations are confirmed usually quickly within it. If Strachey's criterion is redefined as interpretations linked to the transference, it becomes more acceptable but acquires a much vaguer and more general meaning. Secondly, Strachey's stress on the therapeutic importance of introjection of the analyst and his implicit values sits uneasily in his framework, which is orientated to energetics rather than to relationships and values. It seems to me clear that some additional description is needed of what happens in the object relationship of patient and analyst when a successful interpretation is formulated.

What does the analyst do in order to formulate his interpretations? First he tries to discover a theme which will give interdependent relevance to all that the patient is saying and doing. This unifying theme is his explanatory hypothesis, and its discovery requires close application to detail and a good deal of logical thought. Much of this is done preconsciously with an effortlessness which increases with practice. But in fact he can only achieve the necessary analysis and synthesis because he is at various levels of consciousness matching the patient's experiences and modes of operation with his own as he has become aware of them through his capacity for empathy, augmented by his own analysis and by his study. It is evident from the solutions he expresses in his interpretations that he must have asked himself a number of complicated questions: Where does the barrier lie which prevents the patient from being aware of his deeper feelings? Against what impulse is the patient struggling? How does this manifest itself in the relationship? And, above all, what early relationship is he reproducing? By means of such questions the analyst reaches a general conception of what he is going to say. The first act of interpretation normally takes place when he finds an opportunity to formulate his conception as a response to something the patient has said or done. This is the creative act that matches the analyst's idea with the material provided by the patient.

Now R. G. Collingwood, the philosopher and historian, forty years ago made a subtle analysis of the relationship of art and craft which may be usefully applied here. He said that a craftsman has conceived the form he wants to create before he makes it; but what is added to a craft to transform it into an art is that the artist's understanding of what he wants to create changes as he expresses it. Sir Ernst Gombrich has said of art that making comes before matching. But he also emphasizes that any artistic endeavor must start with "an effort after meaning" without which the world would collapse into total ambiguity, and that this effort of necessity follows conventional lines. What I want to point out about the kind of psychoanalytical interpretation that I have so far described is that to a large extent this matching with inner experience, and along conventional lines, comes before making. This is the craft element. The artistic element comes only at the end as the particular point of application is found and the means of expressing the idea presents itself.

This matching activity has significance for the analyst's relationship with his patient. It means that his relationship during this phase is not simply with his patient but also with his own internalized analyst and teachers, and behind them with Freud, with whom he has to enter into an unconscious dialogue before he can formulate his hypothesis. It means that his relationship with his patient, though absorbing, is not all-absorbing.

But there are also interpretations that present themselves to the analyst spontaneously, and occasionally even interpose themselves to his surprise just when he was about to say something else. These belong from the start to the art of psychoanalysis as Collingwood might have defined it. This is where, in Gombrich's terms, making clearly comes before matching, and the analyst suddenly becomes aware of the creative links his ego has forged.

Many writers have alluded to the process. In Letter 130 to Wilhelm Fliess Freud wrote that he probably worked best when he did not really know what he was doing. Theodor Reik emphasized the important role played by surprise. Bion argues the need for the analyst to free himself, so far as is possible, from "memory and desire." Ernst Kris similarly ascribed the resolution in "the good analytic hour" to the silent synthetic function of the patient's ego.

I would like to describe the significance of spontaneity for object relationship and identification. The patient responds spontaneously to both types of interpretation. But the analyst's spontaneity acts to release him from his role as a professional and brings him together with the patient as an individual. It owes its human quality to the fact that it is the sign that not only have impulses based on drives been recognized, but also their amalgamation with fantasies, feelings and values. Values are the individual's encoded judgments on the successful cooperation in the past between the three psychic structures, and they become the preconditions without which drive satisfaction is reduced or rendered impossible. This mediating role of the patient's values is crucial in understanding how therapeutic changes actually come about. Here Strachey's paper stands in an interesting light. On the one hand it correctly extols the far-reaching therapeutic importance of a deep exploration of the transference. But the description of how the image of the analyst based on an archaic superego is eroded provides no detailed explanation of the evocation of warmth, attachment, or the capacity both to identify and to separate.

Various technical consequences follow from this emphasis on spontaneity. Spontaneous exchanges humanize the analytical relationship by the continual interchange of partial identifications. It is this human quality of the relationship which is the antidote to the traumatic quality of transference as much or more than the acceptance of impulses by an analyst who reinforces the benign qualities of the superego. The technique of detraumatization of analysis therefore implies the slow building of interpretative bridges rather than confrontation with the deep unconscious. Of course what is deeply unconscious varies with the illness of the patient. But any attempt to bypass the ego emphasizes the patient's lack of contact with his feelings and increases his ambivalence toward an omnipotent analyst whom he must secretly fear. If bridges are built slowly, the patient can integrate his unconscious fantasies; if he is suddenly confronted, he feels himself split and powerless. The aim of analysis must therefore be to facilitate the patient's awareness and not to force it—as Winnicott emphasized at several points. It makes the development of much resistance (even though at some points it is inevitable) into an indicator of faulty technique rather than a phenomenon to be accepted, since it implies that the patient's defenses have been ignored and not analyzed. It means that repressed memories—at least theoretically— should not be suddenly released but, owing to the analytical preparation, experienced as something the patient has always known. It puts a high value on the analyst's capacity to wait until he has carried the careful process of matching to a stage at which he finds that he can interpret spontaneously, free of any feeling that he is carrying out a wild analysis. This is a difficult demand since he must also avoid traumatizing the patient by his silence. Above all, it suggests that the analyst whose ideal is almost exclusively dominated by the aim of interpreting an uncontaminated transference, perhaps even to the extent that laughter in the session is considered as a technical lapse, may do the patient a great injury. Excessive control may make it even harder than it is to undo the injury inherent in eliciting an intense transference.

What happens between patient and analyst is still mysterious. There can be little doubt that when the analyst gets a clear idea of what unifies the patient's associations and communicates it, something therapeutic happens in the patient. This seems to be true with several varieties of psychoanalytic technique, making them difficult to compare. The personal factors that make a successful analyst may be even more difficult to study. Certainly his analytical capacity in a reductive sense is the first essential. But his ability to reach a creative understanding of the patient's individual needs as ascertained from the changes of his values at different periods of his life, as well as the individual fantasies that underlie them, are crucial and deserve more sophisticated formulation. This is where patient and analyst appreciate the qualities of each other's character, and this is where they make the mutual discoveries that bind them and allow them to part.

Unfortunately I have time for only one illustration, and this has to be a sketch. A deprived and uncontrollably disobedient girl was kept going at convent school by her father's weekly letter, and in later life her sexual object choice was always made on the model of this relationship. But a deeply valued sexual relationship could be sacrificed to her friendship with her lover's wife and family. It could easily be said that it was more important for her to be a member of a family than to have a father figure as a lover, and that a preoedipal fixation was paramount. But the way her ability to sacrifice had come about had followed a complicated path. Of primary importance in it was her father's aunt, a nun who exemplified human goodness more than anyone she knew and whom she loved more than anyone in the world. The one hour a week that they were allowed together at her first school changed the value of her oedipal and preoedipal experience. She learnt to see her father's vulnerability, and she began to love and appreciate austerity. These new values had to be grafted onto those derived from an idealized view of her father, who in her early childhood had been away at the war and who on his return both disappointed and excited her, and a split image of her mother who had been a devout Catholic at the same time as she had had a lover. They were integrated into a dominant fantasy that by the use of her sexuality she would excite a vulnerable man and thereby save the family. The discovery of the importance of these differing values in her current life could only be made piecemeal by unexpected pieces of insight. As the mutual understanding of patient and analyst grew, she became able to modify some aspects of her object choice. Concurrently she began to speak of the comfort of the analytical relationship. It was only in the trusting context of this relationship with the analyst, and after her values had been explored, that she was able to bring forward the crude elements of the oedipus complex and acknowledge her attempts to excite the analyst in the transference.

Value systems are degraded if they are simply interpreted as defenses against impulse. They are mixtures of defenses and of deep emotional satisfactions not always derived directly from aggression or libido. It is in the interpretation of the values of the ego that the wisdom, humanity, and freedom of thought of psychoanalysis are largely experienced. It is in working out unexpected insights in this area that the analysis becomes a friendly relationship and is detraumatized. Perhaps these aspects are little emphasized in the literature, not only because description is difficult, but because this is where the personal and private communication between patient and analyst takes place and therefore where a secret area of value is formed which the analyst wants to protect. It could also be that it is in these areas that adjustments of our theory are liable to take place, so they become a source of danger for our theoretical and professional loyalties.

REFERENCES

Bion, W.R. (1962). *Learning from Experience.* London: William Heinemann.

—— (1970). *Attention and Interpretation.* London: Tavistock.

Collingwood, R.G. (1938). *The Principles of Art.* Oxford: Clarendon Press.

Freud, A. (1966). *Normality and Pathology in Childhood.* London: Hogarth Press.

Freud, S. (1926). Inhibitions, symptoms and anxiety. *Standard Edition* 20:77-175.

—— (1954). Letter 130 to Wilhelm Fliess. In *The Origins of Psycho-Analysis.* London: Imago.

Gombrich, E.H. (1960). *Art and Illusion: A Study in the Psychology of Pictorial Representation.* London: Pantheon Books.

Kris, E. (1956). On some vicissitudes of insight in psycho-analysis. *International Journal of Psycho-Analysis* 37.

Reik, T. (1936). *Surprise and the Psycho-Analyst.* London: Kegan Paul.

Strachey, J. (1934). The nature of the therapeutic action of psycho-analysis. *International Journal of Psycho-Analysis* 15:127-159. Reprinted 50:275-292.

Winnicott, D.W. (1965). *The Maturational Processes and the Facilitating Environment.* London: Hogarth Press.
——— (1971). *Playing and Reality.* London: Tavistock.

III

Difficulties
in the Analyst

8

The Psychoanalyst
as a Person
(1968)

The aim here was to sketch out some of the ways in which
the neglected element of the analyst's personality affects the
course of treatment. It determines what the analyst selects for
interpretation, what he regards as pathological, how far he
can sympathize with the patient's values when they are
different from his own, and at what point the reactions that
help him to understand his patients may turn into a countertransference which becomes an impediment. The outcome
of analysis was seen as not dependent simply on successful
interpretation of transference, but on a successful interaction
between personalities to be judged by the degree to which the
patient could feel free to develop in his own way.

* * *

I do not wish to examine the character of the psychoanalyst as it displays itself in his private life. What I wish to discuss is the variation, dictated by his personality, in the manner of each psychoanalyst's understanding of his patients and the relationship of this variation to the theory of psychoanalytic technique. Though the discussion is in terms of psychoanalysis, it is hoped that it may have some application to other forms of psychotherapy.

The essentials of the most widely practiced psychoanalytic technique were formulated by Freud and received an important systematization through Anna Freud's *The Ego and the Mechanisms of Defence* (1937). Freud regarded the distinguishing feature of psychoanalytic technique as the analysis of the transference. By means of his training analysis the psychoanalyst acquires a sufficient degree of secondary autonomy of his professional function to be able to act like a mirror, in Freud's simile of 1912, to the emotional reactions of the patient in such a way that his attitudes to the analyst can be utilized for the elucidation of the nature of his other relationships.

The psychoanalyst's intellectual operations in each session might be schematized as follows. From the study of the patient's verbal associations and accompanying behavior he postulates connecting ideas. He uses them first to locate the source of the patient's anxiety, next to observe how he attempts to defend himself against the anxiety, then to infer the nature of the underlying impulse seeking discharge. He sees how the struggle between impulse and anxiety manifests itself in the relationship to the analyst and finally makes a communication, based primarily on the nature of the anxiety, which takes all these into account. The diminution of anxiety over an impulse facilitates its freer expression in relation to the analyst, with the result that it can be further understood in terms of its origins. An interpretation is regarded as "confirmed" if the patient brings fresh information to support it, especially a memory which corresponds with an event that has been postulated. This scheme must be regarded as a model which will be modified by the analyst in practice by a number of conscious or preconscious considerations, such as the need to respond to an acutely disturbed patient.

The conclusions derived from careful work along these lines command a high degree of assent from trained judges. The method has enabled covering laws to be formulated over half a century (for instance concerning the displacement of impulses to new objectives or the relationship of symptoms to the forgotten experience of the individual) which, in my view, justify the claim of psychoanalysis to be a scientific discipline. It seems a corollary of this view that Freud's achievement in using scientific method with an unrivaled scope and detail to illuminate the inner life of man could be a turning point in his history.

There is a feature of this discipline, however, the importance of which has been undervalued. One of the covering laws of psychoanalysis is the law of psychic overdetermination—that is, that multiple psychic sources may exist for a single phenomenon of psychic expression. A theoretical consequence of this law is that the psychoanalyst has a choice at each stage among possible interpretations which could be given. Whereas in establishing the covering laws he attempts to provide unitary explanations of multiple phenomena, in the actual technique of psychoanalysis he has to select from multiple explanations of individual phenomena. He does not only make interpretations designed to explain several phenomena; he also has to make complex acts of assessment of the relationship of the phenomena and their determinants to one another. He then has to decide their relative importance both for the etiology of the symptoms and for the technique of interpretation. Sharing an orientation toward the past, his task has sometimes been compared with that of the historian. In spite of the difficulty of historical studies and the varying emphasis given to events by historians, it is important that the possibility of achieving a degree of objectivity of reconstruction and understanding sufficient to justify historical studies has seldom been denied. In history a variety of determinants is accepted without question: social, political, economic, and psychological. It seems to follow, however, from the choice of interpretation open to the psychoanalyst that, as with historical narratives, the path of analytic reconstruction will vary considerably according to the set given by the personality and culture of the analyst. The thesis of this paper is that the significance of the choice of individual paths determined by the psychoanalyst's personality has been insufficiently studied and appreciated in the psychoanalytic theory of technique.

It is true that the effect of variation of personality has often been approached. Freud discussed it both from the point of view of the psychoanalyst's emotional difficulties and from the point of view of his ego. In 1910 he noted that "each analyst's achievement is limited by what his own complexes and resistances permit." In 1933, discussing analytic controversies, he came to the conclusion that the nub of the problem was contained in the old saying *"Quot capita tot sensus"* ("as many heads, so many opinions"). In 1939 Alice and Michael Balint discussed individual differences of technical approach in some detail. They stated that "while formerly belief in the absolute validity of the mirror-like attitude was so firm that contesting it was liable to be regarded as an act of desertion," at the present time "the very possibility of such an attitude is challenged." They concluded, however, that "our patients, with very few exceptions, are able to adapt themselves to . . . these individual atmospheres and to proceed with their own transference almost undisturbed by the analyst's countertransference." The personal response of the psychoanalyst to his patient attracted attention again after the war in a series of important papers. Contributions from D.W. Winnicott (1947), Paula Heimann (1950, 1960), Maxwell Gitelson (1952), and Margaret Little (1957) centered in various ways on the emotional position of the psychoanalyst. His personal responses, if still under the control of his self-scrutiny, were no longer simply excrescences on the polished surface of the mirror; they could be used to bring the mirror into focus. Gitelson and Heimann emphasized that indications could exist from the first contact with a patient that work would proceed better with a different analyst, relating such difficulties chiefly to the interplay of transference and countertransference. Heimann emphasized that the patient consults the analyst for his skill, but she laid appropriate stress on the fact that this skill is "in most intricate and complex ways conditioned by" his personality. Winnicott and Margaret Little emphasized the importance for the patient of experiencing the psychoanalyst as a person capable of a genuine emotional response to him. Of particular relevance to the present theme, Winnicott considered that "the idiosyncratic tendencies of the analyst, as determined by his personal history . . . which make his work different in style and quality from that of his colleagues" should be distinguished from the psychoanalyst's countertransference.

I should like to elaborate the distinction between the individual form and propensities of the analyst's character and the varying emotional responses which he may make to each patient. Winnicott's distinction took up implicitly the difference between the structure of the personality and the

operation of the drives which had been utilized by psychoanalysts with special profit since Freud's publication of *The
Ego and the Id* in 1923.

Clearly generalized attitudes of sympathy or the lack of it
on the part of the analyst to his patient would be likely to
involve tendencies of his character based on his "permanent
neurotic difficulties" (Annie Reich 1951) and might therefore
be described unequivocally in terms of countertransference.
But this does not dispose of all the psychoanalyst's reactions.
Analyst and patient are not only analyst and patient; they are
also individuals with highly integrated, and to a large extent
unmodifiable, systems of values, and the attitude of one to
another expresses not only transference and countertransference but views which remain ego syntonic and
firmly held on reflection. A theory of technique which
ignores the immense influence on the psychoanalytic transac-
tion of the value systems of patient and analyst alike ignores a
basic psychic reality behind any psychoanalytic partnership.
What has to be taken into account is what the Greeks might
have called the ethos of patient and analyst—a word meaning
originally an accustomed seat—in addition to the *pathos* of
more labile reactions. Though the need for suitability of
character between patient and psychoanalyst has received
some formal, and more informal recognition, there seems to
have been little exploration in psychoanalytic literature of its
technical and metapsychological implications. It is not un-
likely that the lack of emphasis on the importance of the
personality of the psychoanalyst may in part be due to the fear
that such a recognition might be misconstrued as a derogation
of the validity of objective methods in psychoanalysis.

Psychoanalysts have long emphasized the importance of
"the therapeutic alliance"—that is, the alliance of the ego of
the patient with the ego of the psychoanalyst, in contradis-

tinction to the regressive dependency stimulated by the transference. The concept of the therapeutic alliance by its name implies the cooperation of two individuals who can each preserve a relative autonomy of the ego in its analytic function. What is less often considered is the variability of the analytic function according to the influence of the individual features of the psychoanalyst's personality. Freud's simile of the mirror remains valid; the essence of analytical influence lies in the psychoanalyst's ability to interpret what the patient is trying, but failing, to communicate to himself in neutral, nonmoralizing terms. Revolutionary in the patient's experience and therapeutically powerful as this attitude in the analyst is, the simile of the mirror requires further examination. Where is the analyst to hold the mirror? And on how many parts of the patient's personality can any psychoanalyst focus it from the position in which he stands? Sometimes the analyst feels that he has been able to formulate the patient's anxieties with special precision. The patient confirms his interpretation with unequivocal agreement and the emergence of repressed memories, which amplify its content. Yet discussion with colleagues who agree with the interpretation seems almost always to reveal that a number of allied, but alternative explanations might have been offered. This is the inevitable consequence of the interplay of differences in personality between psychoanalysts and the psychic overdetermination of the patient's communications.

When the patient visits the psychoanalyst for a consultation, it is not only the psychoanalyst who makes an assessment of the patient—the patient also attempts to make an assessment of the analyst. Though the transference, which begins to be formed before the consultation, has an important share in the patient's subsequent reaction, the capacity of the patient's ego to evaluate is is not paralyzed, as later analysis tends to reveal. Just as a psychoanalyst starts his report on a patient by describing what he looks like, how he moves and how he is dressed, so equally a fund of information about the psychoanalyst reaches the patient—about his capacity to respond, about his tastes and personal attitudes, as displayed, for instance, by the pictures on his walls. Some psychoanalysts seem to regard this as unfortunate and attempt to limit its effectiveness by establishing a so-called "neutral" setting. I believe that the second attitude fails to give adequate credit to human intelligence and the human unconscious. A woman, undoubtedly suffering from paranoid tendencies, gave as her grounds for refusing treatment with a particular psychoanalyst that she could never be analyzed by someone who decorated his consulting room with such bad art. The patient herself had a considerable sensitivity for the visual arts, which she had demonstrated by discerning purchases. One psychoanalyst reported this decision as the arch evidence for the unreasonableness of the patient. A second thought that the perceptiveness which marked her character, perhaps in some respects sharpened by her paranoid tendencies, had made her quickly understand that a psychoanalyst with such taste in pictures would only with great difficulty acquire a sufficient affinity with her own personality to understand it. What criteria can be used to decide which reaction was more realistic—that of the patient, who considered the need for a fundamental sympathy of taste and culture to be a sine qua non of treatment, or that of the psychoanalyst who thought that such difficulties could be resolved by the technical competence of the psychoanalyst in interpreting the transference? The problems involved in understanding a patient from a remote culture—for example, a Japanese—and of estimating the significance and advisability of possible interventions are obvious. The problems involved, and the time which may be consumed, before the set given by his value systems to a psychoanalyst within a particular culture can be accommodated to the set given by the value systems to a patient with a different way of life may also be considerable.

The individual (psychoanalyst or patient) prizes and tries to preserve his value systems because they reflect the attempts at adjustment of the ego and ego ideal to those compromises formed between drive and primitive defense which have acquired permanent structure. Such ideals may take forms compatible or incompatible with the ideals of individual psychoanalysts: propensities toward austerity or luxury, toward the acceptance or nonacceptance of commonly held standards of choice of work, or even of dress, which may be treated by one psychoanalyst as symptoms and by another with toleration. An example might be the longing of a successful academic to become a painter. The choice of each career was determined by ambivalent identifications. It might be maintained that the development of the patient's personality through systematic analysis would ultimately decide the choice of career. But the use of the word *ultimately* would suggest a denial of the importance of what happens in the meantime. In practice it is difficult for the psychoanalyst, when confronted with the imminence of a decisive choice by the patient, not to find that his own system of values inevitably comes into operation. For example, a woman suffering from sexual inhibition was married to a successful husband who suffered from severe unreliability in respect of both his sexual function and many aspects of his character. The result of her first analysis in another country was to give her greater freedom of sexual expression, but she could obtain no satisfaction from her husband, and she started a liaison with a man of lower social class. The first psychoanalyst's interpretations were directed toward stopping the liaison, which was rightly regarded as an acting out of transference fantasies. At this stage it became necessary for the husband's career that the couple should move to England. The patient began a second analysis and commented early that the second analyst's view of the liaison was quite different from that of the first. While he agreed that it expressed transference fantasies, his interpretations acknowledged the increase in the ego's capacity for decision which had accompanied the liberation of her sexuality and sympathized with her need for sexual fulfillment.

Both analysts had some justification for their attitude, and if they had communicated, each might have appreciated the other's reasons for interpreting as he did. "Ultimately" each would almost certainly have given due acknowledgment to both aspects. But the assertion, which is sometimes made, that it follows that the result of analysis would be the same in either case is impossible to prove. It ignores the passage of time and the developments which can intervene through the prolongation, due to the attitude of the analyst, of a particular course of action in the individual patient, or even through the concatenations of chance. In either case, the path taken by the analysis must be affected. A man who, through no fault of his own, had had three psychoanalysts, expressed the negative side of this succinctly: "It is extremely instructive," he said, "to see which of one's personal habits each analyst takes exception to." If psychoanalysis has any effect, it seems impossible to deny that the course of the patient's life may be affected in different ways according to the attitude to a conflict adopted by the analyst.

The permanent orientation of the ego determining both the quality of the psychoanalyst's work and the limits of his capacity for understanding is based partly on "complexes and resistances," but also on legitimate defenses. We interpret as omnipotence of thought the patients' fantasies that analysis will change their character completely, and the same is true of psychoanalysts. The effect of these differences in the ego's defenses becomes evident in the spectrum of patients which individual analysts are willing to treat. Some demand a good standard of intelligence or respond readily to a depth of depression which might arouse anxiety in others, and some treat delinquents or the blind, for instance, where for others such work could progress only with extreme difficulty. I am aware that the border between reactions of the id and the ego is a hazy one. But permanent and well-integrated systems of choice must be accepted as reflecting the structure of the ego, as well as the conflicts which may underlie its final attitude.

The power of the patient's ego to resist the effects of emotional regression in the transference would also seem to be affected by the personality of the analyst as it reveals itself in his concept of the scope and direction which interpretation should take. Classically the regression in the transference has been considered to leave the patient's ego sufficiently intact to be influenced by suggestion only so far as to be induced to consider interpretations, but not so far as to be forced to accept them. Interpretations are never final formulations, and the process of analytical working through could in part be defined as the gradual modification of the interpretations by cooperative work until they satisfy both partners. It has to be admitted, however, that under the conditions of spontaneous clinical response, the point made by Edward Glover in 1931, that an inexact interpretation can be accepted by the patient as a substitute symptom, may sometimes apply. Though the ego can be shown after the analysis, or in a subsequent analysis, to have been in operation, its capacity to reject an inaccurate interpretation can also sometimes be shown to have been temporarily suspended.

The patient's dependency on the analyst's technical mastery must mean that the direction of the analysis is affected by preferences in the psychoanalyst's value system: by his love of rationality or his fascination with the unconscious. This is revealed in his preference for first ascertaining the exact attitude to a problem within the patient's ego or for first interpreting the patient's regressive fantasies, by his tendency to interpret factors inimical to analysis (such as lateness or silence) as due primarily to anxiety or to aggression, by all that is implied in whether the analyst is a man or a woman, by his attitude to the patient's taking important decisions during analysis, by his attitude to marriage as an institution, and so on. It may even be that the variety of value systems acquires social structure in the formation of psychoanalytic schools, so that differences between types of personality and between cultures become secondarily codified in theoretical beliefs.

The process of analysis used to be conceptualized as the working through of the resistances. Resistance is a concept derived from the ego's attitude to warded-off unconscious impulses. It appeared as a particularly dramatic phenomenon when interpretation was concerned primarily with uncovering drive derivatives, with less attention to attitudes of the ego than has been accorded since the development of character analysis by Wilhelm Reich (1928), and subsequently of defense analysis by Anna Freud. The modern technique of analysis has profoundly altered the quality of the patient's response, so that crude repudiation of interpretation plays a comparatively small role. But clinical theory has not fully incorporated the implications of the detailed analysis of the reactions of the ego. The problem of differentiating the patient's resistance from his disagreement with the analyst, based on the feeling that he is being misunderstood, can lead to an impasse in analysis which may not always be fully resolved. The varying emphasis placed by psychoanalysts on differing features in every account of an analysis by a psychoanalyst reveals as equally inevitable the fact that agreement as to appropriate emphasis cannot be relied on between psychoanalyst and patient. Yet where criteria are lacking as to what reactions in the patient can be classified as "resistance" and what attitudes are based on the difference of the patient's opinion from that of the analyst, the situation must be variably assessed by each psychoanalyst. Perhaps psychoanalysts still recognize insufficiently that what is attributed to the patient's "resistance" may sometimes be stimulated by a failure on the part of the analyst to understand, or to respond appropriately to, the patient's needs. For instance, the analysis will be differently experienced by the patient according to whether his personality structure enables him to accept or not the degree and kind of intervention offered by his particular analyst. Patients praise or complain of features of the temperament of the analyst, and the psychoanalyst rightly analyzes the transference significance of their attitudes. Yet the remarks of Paula Heimann and Gitelson on the possible incompatibility of patient and analyst indicate that a residue may remain of differences of temperament which cannot be fully resolved.

It would seem that clinical problems cannot be conceptualized in terms of a theory concerned only with technique. The implication of such an approach would be that the personality of the psychoanalyst can be modified with relative facility to suit a technical recommendation. It is equally true that every psychoanalyst must modify technique to suit the needs of his personality; for instance, his need for expression, communication or humor, his passivity, or his need for reflection.

The theory of the psychoanalytic process which emphasizes the analytic function, to the exclusion of the influence of the psychoanalyst's personality, also ignores the nature of the patient's introjections of the psychoanalyst. Alongside the distorted image of the analyst due to the patient's transference, which is modified by the treatment, goes a considerable perception of his realistic attributes, with the result that the patient identifies with the analyst's real personality and value system. The vicissitudes of these identifications after termination are sometimes difficult to assess in patients who are not professionally involved in psychoanalysis or allied professions, but their importance in those who are can scarcely be doubted.

That the character of the individual psychoanalyst should exert a continual influence on the course and outcome of an analysis stems from the nature of the mind itself. The unconscious cannot be interpreted directly; it can only be inferred from evidence provided by its conscious and preconscious derivatives. Such inferences can be made only from a constant evaluation of the significance of events in the patient's daily life and mental activities. The evaluation of the preconscious involves a detailed discussion of the patient's attitudes to the problems that confront him. To do this the psychoanalyst must make a series of judgments, both in relation to the patient and to third parties. To give an example, a son describes the rigidity and unreasonableness of his father in convincing detail. If the psychoanalyst simply interprets the son's rivalry and aggression in terms of the oedipus complex, the interpretation will lack all conviction for the patient. Only by examining the details of the son's complaints and discussing them is it possible to demonstrate convincingly the operation, in addition to the son's justified complaints, of irrational motives from childhood. But this involves a number of complex value judgments on the real situation both in respect of the patient in his behavior outside analysis and of a third party (his father). To take another example, a newly married man comments on a peculiar circumstance. He is tired after a hard day's work, but the tiredness does not hit him until he puts his key into his front door. The analyst asks if the tiredness could have something to do with coming home: the patient responds with a number of stories showing how controlling his wife is of him. It seems a difficult task for the analyst to open up the patient's dissatisfactions, and at the same time to leave the patient in any genuine doubt as to whether or not the analyst agrees with him in at least some of his realistic criticisms. The degree to which analysis of conscious and preconscious attitudes should be allowed to shade off into discussion of the patient's problems depends upon the theoretical orientation of the psychoanalyst. For those analysts for whom interpretation is orientated to the ego, it seems inevitable for the accurate clarification of the unconscious conflict that the conscious and preconscious derivatives of the unconscious should be fully explored. Other psychoanalysts might dispute the appropriateness of the discussion of the patient's problems of which some analysts approve and consider it a degradation of psychoanalytic technique. In either case it would seem that the emotions experienced by the patient for the analyst must be profoundly altered by the degree to which the psychoanalyst concerns himself with discussion of current problems in realistic terms. The lack of emphasis in the theory given to the analysis of the preconscious and its implications seems to provide further evidence of an avoidance of the more intimate and personal aspects of psychoanalytic technique, in psychoanalytic theory, even though the analysis of the preconscious, in the technique of the majority of psychoanalysts, seems to occupy (in my opinion rightly) a greater proportion of the time than does the interpretation of the unconscious proper. It need hardly be said that such discussion may be understood by the patient in ways which may require a great deal more analysis in terms of unconscious transference from all developmental levels.

To conclude, is there any criterion to judge the success of the personal interaction of patient and psychoanalyst? Though I have tried to show that the psychoanalyst's personality must inevitably influence considerably the direction taken by the analysis, the analytic process initiated in the ego of the patient extends outside his personal contact with the analyst. Just as the success of a teacher may in part be judged by the ability of his students to develop independently, so perhaps the criterion of successful personal interaction between analyst and patient may lie partly in the degree to which the patient shows an ability to make his own synthesis—that is, in part to conduct his own analysis and translate its results into life. This will be seen not only while the contact between patient and psychoanalyst lasts, but particularly after it has ended.

In what way does this criterion of successful interaction differ from the thesis that it is the analytic function of the psychoanalyst and not his personality that counts? The description of the criterion may not differ from one of the generally recognized criteria of successful analysis. What I have tried to suggest in this paper, however, is that the psychoanalytic function cannot be conceptualized in isolation from the personality of the psychoanalyst who exercises it, and that to ignore the influence of his personality results in denials of the realities of the psychoanalytic process for which the patient is liable to pay as a minimum price with loss of time. If psychoanalysis ignores this problem, it diminishes its grasp of the practical and theoretical nature of the method.

REFERENCES

Balint, A., and Balint, M. (1939). On transference and counter-transference. *International Journal of Psycho-Analysis* 20:223-230.

Freud, A. (1937). *The Ego and the Mechanisms of Defence.* London: Hogarth Press.

Freud, S. (1910). The future prospects of psychoanalytic therapy. *Standard Edition* 11.

——— (1912a). The dynamics of transference. *Standard Edition* 12.

——— (1912b). Recommendations to physicians practising psycho-analysis. *Standard Edition* 12.

——— (1923). The ego and the id. *Standard Edition* 22.

——— (1933). New introductory lectures on psychoanalysis. *Standard Edition* 19.

Gitelson, M. (1952). The emotional position of the analyst in the psycho-analytic situation. *International Journal of Psycho-Analysis* 33:1-10.

Glover, E. (1931). The therapeutic effect of inexact interpretation. *International Journal of Psycho-Analysis* 12:397.

Heimann, P. (1950). On counter-transference. *International Journal of Psycho-Analysis* 31:81-84.

——— (1960). Counter-transference. II. *British Journal of Medical Psychology* 33:9-15.

Little, M. (1957). "R"—the analyst's total response to his patient's needs. *International Journal of Psycho-Analysis* 38:240-254.

Reich, A. (1951). On counter-transference. *International Journal of Psycho-Analysis* 32:25-31.

Reich, W. (1928). On character analysis. In *The Psychoanalytic Reader,* ed. R. Fliess. London: Hogarth Press, 1950.

Winnicott, D. W. (1947). Hate in the countertransference. In *Collected Papers.* London: Tavistock, 1958.

9

Personal Attitudes to Psychoanalytic Consultation (1971)

Psychoanalysis seemed often to be recommended without the patient understanding fully what he was embarking on. For instance, some analysts started an analysis before the end of the first consultation hour. This paper was designed to draw attention to some of the pitfalls in consultation, such as the tendency to lay the blame for the ill success of previous treatment on the therapy rather than on the patient's capacity to use it. My emphasis is on a clear understanding between consultant and patient about what is involved, taking full account of the patient's history and the difficulties of analysis. I also emphasize the importance of some trial during the interview of the patient's ability to use interpretation. My ethos of consultation assumes that analysis acts by fostering development not transformation.

*   *   *

To recommend a patient to psychoanalysis is a great responsibility. It implies an enormous investment of hope, often of family involvement, money, and time. Analysis will dominate the patient's psychic life for several years, and he may become more depressed or disturbed and will certainly become more dependent in the course of treatment. The analysis, and the powerful effects of the transference, may seriously affect marital relationships or the choice of a partner or a career. An underlying conflict of value systems between patient and analyst may cause a permanent discontent which the patient is unable to articulate and which may force him to make painful psychic adjustments that can only gradually be thrown off after the analysis is ended. Failure of the analysis may result in the impoverishment of the personality of the patient and, if too often repeated, of the analyst. Similarly, if the analyst, confronted with what appears to be a stalemate, forces termination before the patient is fully ready and willing, this can also be destructive to both. The psychoanalyst is left with a sense of failure and guilt, the patient feels the rejected victim of a broken home. In some cases analysis lasts for twenty years or more, usually with the patient changing analysts several times. Successfully analyzed patients not uncommonly want to return, and no one knows in what proportion of cases the habit of analysis, once established, cannot be permanently broken. It is remarkable that so little attention has been paid in the psychoanalytic literature to the criteria on which analysis is recommended.

When a patient seeks a psychoanalytic consultation, he presents the analyst with a problem at the center of his life. He comes in a crisis in his relationship to his life, whether he brings this overtly as the final instance of a repetitive failure or as a self-critical depression, or in the guise of symptoms, which are the acute expression of permanent unconscious conflicts. Since only a partial understanding of a life problem can be reached at consultation, since the concept of cure for problems rooted in the character structure is only partially applicable, since psychoanalysis is not an entity in itself, but a complex relationship between two individuals whose understanding of one another will inevitably also be partial, it is clearly inappropriate that it should be recommended like a medicine. Recommendations of this kind are not infrequently made however, especially by doctors who are not psychoanalysts or by inexperienced analysts.

If someone's difficulties are rooted in his life and character, more than a recommendation will be needed for him to understand how psychoanalysis can help him. Here a problem arises. He will need discussion of his situation and of what may or may not be expected from analysis. But as analysis works by giving access to unconscious emotions, this understanding cannot be given by intellectual means alone. It can only be fully grasped by the actual experience of analysis, but at this point the patient comes only for consultation. He has therefore to get an experience of analysis within the framework of the consultation. This is the essence of consultation, and achieving it is a delicate procedure. The consultant cannot and should not conduct a miniature analysis. If he did, it would either overwhelm the patient or attach him too much to his person at the expense of the smooth evolution of the transference to his eventual analyst. But successful consultation can offer enough tentative explanation and interpretation to give the patient a glimpse of the emotional and intellectual processes involved without unduly seducing him. It is primarily the quality of the rapport formed as a result which will enable patient and consultant to judge if the patient can make further use of this type of experience.

How is this experience to be given? The technique of analysis and the technique of consultation are not the same. The aim of analysis is to free the patient to make his own decisions. Consultation inevitably has more of an advisory role, however much we may try to bring the patient to his own point of decision. After all, even the consultant's recommendation to another analyst is loaded with control on the basis of his assessment of factors of which the patient has little or no awareness, such as his assessment of prognosis or of the capacities of other psychoanalysts. Its aim is a plan of action to be discussed in rational terms at the end of the sampling procedure of consultation. Consultation must therefore be directed primarily to the functioning ego. So in a sense must analysis. But there is more than one psychoanalytic technique and a considerable variation in the degree to which different psychoanalysts approach problems from the standpoint of the id or of the ego. If the patient is to commit himself to a procedure lasting an indeterminate number of years, after which, for better or worse and sometimes both, he may never be the same, it is only fair that he should do so with his powers of judgment as fully in operation as possible. He will greatly appreciate the care which is taken to ensure that he makes his decision without being pressured. This is especially important as the power of the transference, once analysis is started, to hold the patient in an unsatisfactory situation is not to be underrated. This attempt to give the patient as full a freedom of choice by rational means as possible is in fact the first way in which he glimpses the ethos and method of psychoanalysis. The difference is that the aim of consultation demands that this emphasis on the conscious functioning of the ego should be sustained and paramount. Even more than in analysis there should be no playing of the doctor game or any of its variants, like the silent analyst.

This orientation toward the ego also enables another aspect of psychoanalysis to be demonstrated. The patient needs to know that psychoanalysis is sensible and that decent analysts are sensible, not mad. Even more, he needs to understand that psychoanalysis can make good sense of what he feels as madness and that it will not at the first breath compound the madness with the omnipotent symbolic or "deep" interpretations which he may expect or consciously hope for.

All this implies that if something of the function of the symptoms in preserving the stability of the patient can be grasped by the consultant and communicated, this will be the best demonstration of all of the rationality and depth of insight of psychoanalysis. To take a simple example, a woman architect in her late twenties broke down with crying attacks and psychic paralysis when insufficiently supported by her male superior. She had a good personality and was successful in her work, but she had got where she had in order to personify her father's ideal of his own father. The question was "Where is she now?" It is surely better to verbalize this to the patient and to discuss her need for emotionality, which her parents suppressed in her, than to interpret the contributions to her breakdown from the oedipus complex. This I take as obvious. But it is in practice the hardest test of a consultant to wrest the contribution of the ego regularly and clearly from the disguises produced by the patient's fear of his own unconscious aspirations. It is not merely the emotional difficulty involved in sustaining the attempt to obtain the rational and human from people who occasionally present themselves in a bad light. There may also be a difficulty in combining a capacity to listen, to respond appropriately, and to observe with the intense intellectual activity necessary to construct a coherent picture of the patient's life pattern and to formulate it, or at least begin to formulate it, as a living response in the time available—as may sometimes be necessary. However, I believe that with time and a capacity to wait it is possible in most cases for a consultant to gain enough information without undue effort for a fairly convincing understanding of the patient's presenting problem in the context of his life from childhood to the present day.

This poses an administrative and technical problem of how much time it is necessary to allot for a consultation. To some extent this must depend upon the taste and temperament of the consultant and, to a lesser extent, upon the capacity and needs of the patient. A few patients are too inhibited to make use of an extended first interview, but this will not occur very frequently with an experienced interviewer. Whatever the time, it must obviously be enough for the patient to feel that some contact has been made, otherwise the consultation may not be continued. To set aside a session may be enough for a first interview in some instances, but it is dangerous to allow a period which may prove frustrating or in some cases may be too short to deal with unexpected developments. The aim should rather be to give the patient time to state his problem fully enough to be able to wait peacefully for the next interview, if another interview is necessary. The majority of patients come to consultation in a state of anxiety and tension. The functioning of their ego has been impaired by regression, so it tends to operate under increased pressure from the primary process, that is, on an all-or-none basis. Behind their politeness, their unsatisfied fantasies, libidinal or aggressive, contribute to the events of the interview. This means that for the patient to feel really satisfied with the consultation, he must have discharged his tension and reached the feeling that he has said all that he needed to say at that particular time and that what he has said has registered. This needs a good deal of time. For my own speed of working, fifty minutes is rarely adequate, though to allot longer may on occasion be a counsel of perfection for a busy psychoanalyst. I cannot agree with the view (Glover 1949) that a longer period than an hour imposes an excessive strain on the patient, except in the rare cases already mentioned. The vast majority of patients come with a great load of accumulated tension and do not find that time spent talking about their problems passes slowly, as later analysis shows. On the other hand, the consultant has to consider himself too, and he should not become the masochistic victim of compulsive delayers. I find that if I allow an hour and three quarters, I can complete most consultations or at least reach a satisfactory stage for breaking them off. To allot two hours allows ample time for making a few brief notes at the end. When I review the information I have gleaned in this time, however, I frequently find important gaps, and I may have to see the patient a second or third time to continue the assessment and think over my recommendation in the light of further developments. After the initial consultation it is usually possible to fit the patient into a fifty-minute schedule.

A consultation, then, is an extended private talk between analyst and patient in which the analyst tries to get the feel of the patient's personality and to give him the feel of the character of psychoanalysis and of how a psychoanalyst may employ his personality to enrich his professional role.

How the patient judges this may be revealed in his subsequent analysis. A good consultation should stimulate as little as possible the feeling that the patient who is referred to a second analyst is being fobbed off with second best, but allow the analysis to get under way without impediment. However, the personality of the consultant should make a sufficiently positive impression to be valued for future reference if difficulties occur. It may well be, however, that the immense initial transference of the patient to the consultant in fact makes a more lasting imprint than we usually allow for in our egocentricity when we analyze patients who are referred to us.

Advising patients who have already had one or more analyses is an important and difficult part of a consultant's work. The deficiencies of the earlier analysis are always consciously or unconsciously exposed, and the consultant's feelings of professional rivalry are easily stimulated. It is important not to be too easily drawn in to criticisms of the previous analyst, even when a gross failure seems to have occurred. What is more relevant is to disentangle the repetitive elements in the patient's history (without using them to blame the patient for the analyst's failure) and to assess the significance of the patient's attitude to his previous analyst for the aims of the present consultation. For example, a patient may present criticisms, perhaps valid, of an analyst who has helped him considerably and whose advice he is using in coming to the particular consultant. Interpretation of these positive elements may clarify the degree of the patient's confusion of feeling in his present crisis or be the indicator of a possible underlying paranoid process.

I shall try to outline some of the main criteria which a consultant can use, or try to use, in making referrals and some of the pitfalls he may encounter. In this attempt I know that I shall not succeed in giving more than a sketchy and personal presentation. Worse, much of it may turn out to be an unpleasant combination of the dogmatic and the banal. My excuse is that it has taken me a long time to orientate myself to the tasks of consultation and that my most common mistakes are of an elementary kind.

The first thing I set out to do is to make contact with the patient about his problem. I regard psychoanalytic consultation as a traumatic event in a patient's life, and I do not think he should be further traumatized by being left almost entirely on his own to make a start, frightened and sometimes ashamed. Some sort of bridge to shared experience is usually possible without guiding the patient's responses. This can be quite slight, such as "I have heard a bit about your problem from Dr. So-and-So, but I would like to hear about it directly from you." The quicker the patient is put at his ease, the freer the communication and the fuller the consultation. This also is obvious, and I would not stress it unless I believed that the ethos of the detached analyst—or the analyst as a mirror—were sometimes used as a cover for sadism.

The consultation inevitably starts with certain preformed ideas in the consultant's mind. He may have had telephone contact with the patient. Probably he has already had experience of the sort of cases the referring doctor sends: he starts with some suspicion of the general practitioner who tends to send cases on his own rather than the patient's initiative or with confidence in the woman gynecologist, in some trouble herself, who makes her cases sound worse than they are, and he knows the reliable colleague who may want a considered opinion on the relative of one of his patients with a difficult character problem. Above all, he gets certain impressions as the patient enters the room and begins to talk. None of these impressions or preliminary ideas are to be discounted. But it is even more important that they should be carefully balanced in the consultant's mind in the light of the total interview. He must beware of judging by impression, even though he will rightly sometimes allow his impression to overrule his judgment. One sometimes is convinced of the correctness of a feeling when one's apparent reason urges one differently. Nonetheless, to rely too much on impression is to ask for difficulties. Perhaps the most common pitfall is to blame the ignorance or ineptitude of other doctors for the failure of previous treatment and instead to believe the patient's assurances of his serious intentions. So equally, patients who present themselves poorly may demonstrate by their history that they have a greater reliability than they allow themselves to show.

A consultation is an interaction between two personalities, previously unknown to each other, in which the patient is trying to express himself on topics of great emotional resonance. There is therefore scope for the unpredictable to occur and for errors of judgment to be made—that is, for irrational response to the patient's transference. I believe that it is wise for any psychoanalyst to remember this before accepting a patient for analysis, no matter who the consultant has been. This contrasts with the advice sometimes given to make the preliminary interview as short as possible or even to convert it into an analytic session. It does however have the advantage of ensuring from the start that the analyst acts on his own judgment and that this can be seen by the patient.

What is to be evaluated at consultation, and how is this to be done? But first is there any need to evaluate a great deal at consultation? If the patient has "a fairly reliable character," can respond with nondelusional transference, wants psychoanalysis, and has the money to pay for it, can the decision not be left to him? On this view psychoanalysis is the treatment of choice for the moderately ill, and consultation consists largely in excluding psychosis and in subsequent referral. This comes near to the view of psychoanalysis as a medicine which I have already criticized. Psychoanalytic diagnosis must of necessity be more sophisticated than psychiatric diagnosis. It depends upon a complex assessment of defenses and motives and reaches a richer, and deeply relevant, picture of the personality stretching far back into the patient's history. Most importantly, it recognizes the strength of the compulsion to repeat patterns of relationship inside and outside analysis and can therefore make some attempt at a prognosis of how an analysis will run. This attempt may be inexact, but at least it alerts the potential analyst to some of the possible complications. Besides, the patient knows too little of such possible impediments and needs and deserves the opportunity to interact with the consultant's experience, for instance, to discuss his difficulty in making full use of opportunities he may value. If he is to embark on analysis, or to decide against it, or to begin a course of analytic psychotherapy with full conviction of the wisdom of his choice, he needs to have defined as far as possible the nature of his crisis and its place in his life history.

It follows that the essential factor to define at consultation is the nature of the patient's motivation in its widest sense. His sustained and realistic engagement with analysis is clearly the most important requirement for success. In fact, however, the patient's motivation, even at a conscious level, is the factor most consistently overlooked in making a referral to a consultant. What commonly brings the patient is the pressure of his immediate suffering, usually on himself, but not infrequently on his doctor or his family. But in any case his conscious motivation, whether for analysis or against it, is only a partial indicator of his unconscious motivation. It is his unconscious motivation which has to be determined—the repressed wish, so to speak, behind the manifest content of his presentation and the relevance of this wish to the present crisis in his life. Ideally, therefore, the whole illness must be scrutinized to elicit and make clear to the patient the nature of the motive which has brought him. This is, of course, an impossible task, requiring not merely a whole analysis but subsequent reflection on it. It may well be that the consultant may suspect motivation which he may think it unwise to communicate—say, the desire to become acceptable to a mother for whom the child was fundamentally unacceptable. But if he attempts the task of a thorough assessment, the whole quality of the consultation will change, and what can be communicated to the patient will emerge more clearly— for instance, the possible difficulties that a woman may have to guard against in sustaining a marriage or in becoming a mother in view of the history of her own relationship with her mother.

To reach such an assessment clearly requires success at a number of stages. The first requirement is to assess the patient's desire to communicate and his capacity to develop communication to a deeper level. The emotional level of what he says must be compared with the emotional level which the consultant infers for his illness. The "illness" is of course essentially the product of a character problem, and the evaluation of the symptoms can be made accurately only on the basis of the evaluation of the character defenses. A successful professional man comes to consultation on his wife's initiative. He does not feel any need of it. His complaint is that her constant criticism is getting him down. He adds that he has even come to believe that he has "feet of clay" professionally and he recognizes that he is being overtaken by younger men. It emerges that his wife is a substitute for his father, who was literally and metaphorically a wholesale butcher, and that his professional self-doubt has become accentuated since his wife has had quarrels with a professional adviser in a field symbolically related to his own. In considering this man's problem, it will be necessary to evaluate the total extent of the masochism in his character and not merely the sexual masochism which made him marry her. Only when the relative balance of his justified self-criticism, of his turning of his aggression against himself, and of his sexual masochism are determined can the danger of a serious depression be estimated.

Some of the patient's character defenses—such as turning of aggression against the self, or of denial, or isolation of affect—can be interpreted immediately and the patient's response noted. The discussion of the life pattern also affords an opportunity for pointing out some of the patterns of repetition or unconscious equations and identifications, and observing the nature of the analytical engagement which usually follows. In this connection the significance of organic illness is not to be neglected, either as an indicator of psychological crisis or for the evaluation of fixation points. Such comments or interpretations as are made can still be general in nature and within the capacity of the conscious ego to appreciate. If they are not too "wonderful" or startling, they need not interfere unduly with a subsequent analysis by another analyst. If the patient's power of communication is blocked, even transference interpretations can be given provided they are made in general terms not designed to rape the patient for analysis (and for the consultant) by overwhelming his ego with unconscious impulse. A woman, married to a perpetually tired man with a low sperm count, presents with depression because she has not conceived a second child. It is not necessarily traumatic to relieve her hesitation in speaking by telling her that it may be difficult for her to discuss her sexual problems with her husband with another man. On the other hand, she might be disturbed in a way she might find difficult to control if she were told that she could not speak to the consultant because she was afraid of falling in love with him.

The overall concept of motivation represents the final availability of motive after the inhibiting forces of the illness, notably rigidity of defenses and degree of traumatization, have been allowed for.

The indications for the future also depend on another balance of forces. If the motivation is to be assessed primarily on the history of past struggles against regression, then the potential outcome has to be assessed in terms of the feasibility of change within the patient's life situation. Failure to recognize the difficulties of the life situation sufficiently is in fact one of the important reasons for which the final therapeutic results of analysis sometimes disappoint when contrasted with the analytic results in terms of illumination of psychopathology. Is a full analysis really indicated for the woman, married to her tired husband, when she does finally conceive her second child and still complains of depression? Other balances may require more subtle decisions: for instance, the need of analysis of an émigré with a possibility of continuing to work in the country for some years, but under the thumb of a discontented wife who looks forward to their return to their own country—and so on.

I will list a few of the types of patient and situations of which I am wary. I am deliberately suspicious of charming patients, and even of "very good cases for analysis." If one is charmed, one's critical judgment is lulled. Besides, the ability to charm in a state of distress may indicate either excessive narcissism or despair, and how often can one really meet a very good case for analysis? When we really achieve splendid results, what was the trick? While the quality of the analysis in these cases was usually good, the result may well have been facilitated by a considerable rapport. I hesitate with patients who try to make unrealistic arrangements, and I do not think that analysts should compound arrangements which will turn psychoanalysis into a burden, or to break down, or cause the patient to hate it. A young mother in the suburbs should not be expected to park her baby five times a week to come to town. An analyst who encourages a patient to change his place of residence and work for analysis is either brave or foolhardy. An analyst who charges the patient more than he can afford for four or five "necessary" sessions a week instead of adjusting his therapy to what the patient can pay misses the wood for the trees. Psychoanalysis (as it seems to me) is a way of understanding people, and whether the patient sits or lies or takes a walk round the town like Gustav Mahler is to some extent peripheral. Similarly, the analyst who consents to treat a patient out of his diminishing capital is onto a bad bet, especially with a masochistic patient. What a temptation to express his resentment by not getting better, until all his capital is exhausted! I do not like patients with only one symptom: the lack of capacity for varied forms of displacement implies a near-delusional mechanism. Similarly a psychosomatic complaint without adequate additional conflicts or anxieties makes me suspicious of the patient's power to sustain analysis. I do not believe all that has been written about the relationship of ulcerative colitis to psychosis, but I am inclined to believe with de Boor (1966) that it is characteristic of bronchial asthmatics to hold their love objects at an intermediate distance, neither allowing them to come close nor to go, and I do not welcome this form of transference. Like others I regard hypochondriasis with suspicion. While hypochondriacal patients clearly have serious problems with projected and reintrojected aggression and may have great difficulty over making stable love relationships, including analytic relationships as a result, I do not regard hypochondriasis as necessarily an indicator of near psychosis. I will end this list with the most dogmatic statement of all. While I believe that patient psychotherapeutic work can greatly help severely disturbed patients and not infrequently transform their lives, I believe that the greatest pitfall of analysis is an excessive belief in our power to reconstitute the character.

The best results are still generally to be obtained with those who, in Freud's description, "have a fairly reliable character" to start with.

There remains a class of patient who "needs" analysis, because he is making someone else's life or analytic treatment impossible, but cannot see it. Very occasionally there may seem to be no alternative but to send them to analysis as the older child analysts tended to send a child. An example would be the husband in a double second marriage characterized by constant rows which were provoked on each side. The rows often centered on the husband's sexual seduction of his children, all of whom required psychiatric help. In spite of her propensity to provoke rows the stepmother's concern for the children was genuine, but she could not get her point of view through to the perverse father. In general such solutions do not work. As soon as the second analysis begins, a surprising amount of projection on the part of the spouse who advocated it becomes revealed. Besides, to persuade someone into analysis by telling him what a mess he is in when he does not quite believe it provokes profound resentment and resistance.

However, a more common problem than that of pitchforking patients into analysis is the question of how to keep them out of it. They feel ill and ask for treatment, and if one analyst does not provide it they can go to the next. It may be agreed at once that a person in distress, or suffering from a psychiatric illness, who asks for help has to be helped, and that in general, for the type of patient who consults a psychoanalyst, some deeper understanding of his illness is the help he needs. In this sense he needs psychoanalysis as I have already defined it: a particular way of understanding people. But in a technical sense this definition is not discrete enough. Patients are differently treated if they discuss their problems, or sit in a chair and engage in an analytic exchange twice a week for a year or two, or lie on a couch three, four, or five times a week for years on end while their unconscious fantasies about the analyst sitting behind them are consistently explored and related in detail to the totality of their problems in life. It is difficult to define the difference, but perhaps one valid generalization is that patients in skilled psychotherapy seem to be spared a great deal in suffering and in regression and to do remarkably well on it. In Freud's day there was no acceptable alternative to full psychoanalysis. Today, with a greatly extended social and possibly psychological range of patients, psychoanalysts are experienced in applying analysis to groups and individuals. It is also a naive analyst who does not bear in mind that therapies not based on interpretation also have their successes and will never consider recommending them.

The main object of consultation therefore defines itself as making a tentative estimate of a feasible aim for treatment. To do this it attempts to answer a series of questions.

First: Is this a patient who ought to have a full analysis from the start, or is he someone who may not be able to use this fully, and with whom, therefore, either some completely different form of therapy is indicated (like relaxation therapy for a tense, elderly obsessional of limited intelligence with a history of depressive breakdown), or a form of analytic psychotherapy which does not prejudice later analysis should this be found to be indicated?

Next: Who is the sort of analyst who will be able to understand this patient's problem? The answer here must be intuitive, but some similarities of character agree and some do not. It is not implied that an inhibited violinist has to be recommended to an intensely musical analyst who may share in some degree a virtuoso's obsessionality. But the perverse

husband who seduced his children might have been considered suitably placed with an experienced woman analyst with
special experience of child analysis.

Thirdly: How can the patient's needs be matched with his
financial resources? How can the dilemma be resolved of the
young academic (say) with a transvestite perversion who
rightly feels he needs a full analysis in spite of his slender
means? Should he be allowed to go to a clever but newly
qualified analyst four or five times a week at a low fee, or
should he be sent to someone more experienced at a higher fee
twice a week?

The answer to this must depend very much on individual
judgment and the availability of analysts. But with cases of
unusual difficulty it seems to me justified to remember that no
analyst did his best work with his first set of patients and that
intractable cases will adversely affect his morale for many
years. This of course raises the question of what is psychoanalysis in another form. Clearly a patient may get more
psychoanalysis in the sense of analytic understanding sitting
in a chair twice a week with someone who understands him
easily than lying on a couch five times a week with an analyst
who is hard put to it to grasp the continuity.

The consultation is at an end when I feel satisfied that I
have a reasonable grasp of the patient's problem and when I
feel that he can feel satisfied with what I have to tell him.
Since a whole analysis is not enough to understand a person's
problems, this point is determined by affective indicators.
But affects are, after all, the arbiters of all our judgments.
Having formed a judgment, I like it to be shared with
whoever else may be involved—certainly with the patient's
doctor whenever possible. He can be of great help to patient
and analyst in a crisis and, especially, at holiday time. If one

gives a patient the name of a colleague, the colleague may be inhibited and chary of offering interpretations, or he may give interpretations, in which case he is liable to become the object of the patient's transference fantasies. If one is lucky in finding a friendly general practitioner, who is in no sense a rival, he may be able to handle the patient on common sense lines without undue transference complications. Moreover, the reputation of psychoanalysis will not be damaged by his subsequent discovery of crises handled without his knowledge. The general practitioner can also be of great help in illuminating the family background or even in bringing medical information which the psychoanalyst may find of importance in his assessment.

The other people involved may be relations. If a relative pays for the treatment, he deserves to know a little of what he is paying for. I ask a wife who can not pay out of earnings to discuss it with her husband. With a young adult (I do not see children) I sometimes ask for permission to discuss at least the general nature of the problem and its implications with the parents.

Finally, I do not think that the patient should have to commit himself under pressure. If the potential analyst is oneself, it is especially important to make as sure as is possible without driving the patient away that he can have a graceful way out of it.

REFERENCES

de Boor, C. (1966). *Zur Psychosomatik der Allergie ins besondere des Asthma Bronchiate.* Bern: Huber; Stuttgart: Klett.
Glover, E. (1949) *Psycho-Analysis.* London: Staples Press.

10

The Identity of
the Psychoanalyst
(1976)

This introduction to a symposium defined two contradictions which need to be resolved before a psychoanalyst can acquire a professional identity. The first is that psychoanalysis is in the end a cure for the incurable. The second is that the difficulty of the technique and the authority of the masters, from Freud to the training analyst, make it a hard task for students of mature age to achieve originality. It describes some of the difficulties which typically lie in the path of becoming a psychoanalyst.

* * *

The identity of the psychoanalyst was the subject of the Haslemere Conference organized by the International Psychoanalytical Association in February 1976. Two papers were precirculated, one by Edward Joseph, currently president of the Association, the other by Daniel Widlocher, at that time its secretary. The abstracts of these two papers printed here have been approved by their authors. The paper that follows them (slightly altered for publication) opened the discussion.

ABSTRACT OF PAPER BY EDWARD JOSEPH

Identity is a relatively new concept in psychoanalysis—it is not mentioned in Fenichel's compilation—and Joseph starts by reviewing its use. He summarizes this in two main ways:

1. It refers to the establishment of a stable, unique, personal self-representation, including a person's sexual identity, which coalesces by the end of the adolescent period.
2. It refers to a social identity. This springs from an inherent sense of continuity with one's past which includes the development of relationship with the community.

The psychoanalyst comes to psychoanalytic education with a well-developed sense of personal identity, but not yet of a social identity as a psychoanalyst. The analyst's training analysis "has as its goal the working through of personal problems," and this is the unique feature of psychoanalytic education. But this is supplemented by an academic education and a practical apprenticeship which bring the opportunity, not only to work with others but to feel at one with them. This development includes the normal processes of identification and sense of continuity of knowledge by means of which any scientist becomes a member of a professional group, receiving the sanction of society.

If the science is new and is not accepted, the sense of identity comes from the close identification of the group with its inspiring leader. This was the situation in Freud's original circle, and there was then no doubt as to the nature of psychoanalytical identity. The paradox of present-day psychoanalysis is that the success of the new ideas has been so great and these ideas have been applied so widely that they have lost their uniqueness. There has also grown up a wide diffusion of principles and practices throughout the world. The psychoanalytic organizations tend to become the codifiers of rules, with potential struggles for power over the determination of those rules. The International Psychoanalytical Association, which with its long history might help in this, is for most psychoanalysts a somewhat shadowy organization.

"What is psychoanalysis?" asks Joseph.

For Freud it was an investigative tool, a theory, and a form of therapy. Most psychoanalysts today regard themselves primarily as therapists applying a theory which has acquired the sanctity of scientific truth and immutability. "The investigative use of psychoanalysis," he says, "has been regarded as the province of the very few."

What part of theory is in fact basic and what is subject to alteration? What is basic is: First, that there are unconscious mental processes and a barrier against their becoming conscious; second, that there is a continuity in the psychic life (as Rapaport emphasized), and finally, the assumption of a psychic energy, which, while derived from somatic sources, is different from physical energy. What is not well recognized is that much has been evolved from these basic concepts which could be changed or done away with without affecting them or affecting the use of psychoanalysis as an investigative tool or therapy. In fact this has occurred over the seventy-five years of psychoanalytic theory, but many psychoanalysts act as though the theories which guide them were unchanged. They also disagree about what changes can and should take place.

It is these disagreements which chiefly lie at the basis of controversy, for instance as to how far the mental phenomena of early periods of life not easily subject to direct observation can be reconstructed. In psychoanalysis, Joseph concludes, the nature of evidence to support explanatory hypotheses and assumptions is a problem that has not been adequately solved. It tends to depend on "consensual validation," in which unresolved identification with the training analyst may sometimes play a part rather than experimental verification. These unresolved cross-identifications may then become institutionalized. In this way the psychoanalytic graduate may receive a one-sided education, and opposing camps be formed, with failure to communicate and resultant splits.

Passing from theory to therapy, what are the basic therapeutic criteria that distinguish psychoanalysis? Here Joseph answers: the use of free association, the attempt to reconstruct earlier mental prototypes, to recognize and interpret transference and countertransference defenses, to be objective and to change hypotheses that are not confirmed.

What then is psychoanalytic identity? Just as the identifications of the adolescent period give way to a sense of identity as an adult, so the psychoanalytic educational period is marked by a succession of identifications with the training analyst, supervisors, teachers, colleagues, which gives way to an identity as a psychoanalyst. "The identity of a psychoanalyst is marked internally by the capacity to think, feel and react as a psychoanalyst." Some years in which the psychoanalyst practices mainly psychoanalysis allow the precarious psychoanalytical identity to become autonomous, though continuous efforts of self-analysis and education are necessary throughout life to maintain its autonomy. It is normally buttressed by entry into a psychoanalytical society, which is itself part of a wider organization. It may be invaded by the facile use of analysis where the observational data may not be adequate for the method, for instance in politics. It may also be invaded or aided by the facilitating or hostile attitudes of the social and political milieu. Psychoanalytic identity is aided by the privilege of teaching psychoanalysis.

In summary, the identity of the psychoanalyst is that of a scientist who has knowledge that may be therapeutically or epistemologically effective in a wider range of human behavior. It includes a high degree of integrity in the search for truth as well as the moral commitment to its acceptance whatever its nature may be. It involves commitment to the best in the Hippocratic tradition and the best in the scientific tradition.

ABSTRACT OF "PSYCHOANALYSIS TODAY: A PROBLEM OF
IDENTITY" BY DANIEL WIDLÖCHER

Widlocher is not sure whether there really is a crisis in psychoanalysis today or whether what appear to be the elements of crisis are not merely the dynamic factors in our evolution to which we do not yet know how to respond. If there is a crisis, then its manifestations are variable. For instance, some groups face the dangers of rapid growth with increased responsibilities to the outside world and accompanying dangers of dilution, while others suffer from isolation. If there is a crisis, it is one of identity, and it comes in fact from the success of psychoanalysis and its integration with the culture, so that reference to Freud is no longer the special perquisite of the trained analyst. Our identity rests on the psychoanalytic experience, which has been identified with the Freudian discovery; the problem is how to hold onto this identity while accepting its displacement onto new applications as proof of its vitality.

Certainly every variation in technique casts doubt upon the results obtained by it—a problem which Freud raised in 1912 in relation to Jung. In order to tolerate our disagreements, we have to be sure of one thing—the reliable transmission of something the unconscious dimensions of which are largely indefinable: that is, the psychoanalytic experience. It is not surprising that it is disputes about training which most directly threaten the cohesion of psychoanalytic groups. Beyond the struggles for influence and power, it is because it is training which in a very direct way alters the feeling of identity. To recognize ourselves as psychoanalysts—that is, to be satisfied that we take part in a common experience—is the necessary condition for us to communicate to each other the results of this experience and to accept our divergencies.

Our identity rests in a similar way on our work, on what we do with our patients, though this is also hard to describe. "To arrange for a certain interhuman encounter, to encourage and to spot in this situation quite specific processes, to communicate certain of its elements so that the patient feels free and secure when facing the instincts and internalisation processes"—these three elements avoid any closer definition of the psychoanalytic process which was originally defined only in terms of the neurotic conflict. Today we see the essence as the analytic encounter, which is no longer seen as a way of inducing regression and transference, but as a more open-ended game in which patient and analyst find their own style. To be a psychoanalyst is no longer so much to accomplish a certain task as to offer a new method of relationship.

However, the fact that psychoanalysis has to deal with structured resistances must not be obscured in favor of a definition which might refer to the transactions between the patient's and the analyst's systems of wishes. It can be argued that no matter what the vicissitudes of the process are with respect to the patient, what lays the foundation of the psychoanalyst's identity is the nature of the psychic work which is demanded from him. But a peculiar silence surrounds the description of the difficulties we meet in our practice. We often refer to the difficulties arising from countertransference, but it is necessary to distinguish between the special difficulties involved in each individual's need to repeat and the general difficulties arising from the demand that the psychoanalyst's work exerts on our usual method of mental functioning.

"To psychoanalyze means, in the first place, to fight the enticements of the encounter. To be able to give maximum interest and availability without yielding to the demands of the patient to establish a defensive compromise in order to preserve the relationship of the transference regression. Another difficulty arises from the power of fascination exercised by the patient's narration and the world, real or imaginary, which he lets us see. We must give up . . . using only . . . empathy . . . in order to grasp . . . the unconscious mechanisms. More deeply, it is about the transference holds, and therefore counter transference ones, that we have to be watchful. Finally, to behave as a psychoanalyst is to be able to develop a specific method of mental functioning which does not come naturally to us." This is why our practice as analysts cannot be compared with any other practice or scientific undertaking. For this reason our basic practice, far from being made easier, on the whole, in spite of advances, is as difficult as it was at the time of the Freudian discoveries.

The part-time psychoanalyst. In Europe more than 70 percent of psychoanalysts have professional activities separate from psychoanalytic activity proper. Are these analysts, who conduct psychotherapy, or teach, or work in administration still psychoanalysts in the performance of these tasks? The answer generally given is that the psychoanalytic attitude gives these tasks a new dimension, and the analyst continues to use his specific method of mental functioning. But it has to be recognized that, in general, to put this method of functioning into operation is more difficult in these situations; the time given by the analyst to psychoanalysis proper is necessary to the nurture of this function. It seems to Widlöcher somewhat excessive to say that the part-time psychoanalyst retains a specific mental attitude in his other tasks. These tasks are very varied. To assess a student, say, or to examine the budget of an institution demand different mental attitudes; a splitting between several methods of mental functioning, or at least a balance, establishes itself. Everyone has some such balances. To study these equilibria, and the individual variables at play, would assume that our identity rests in fact on the awareness of a particular type of mental functioning and not on a collective ideal. To study the identity of the psychoanalyst also demands the study of the way in which the psychoanalyst lives and what way social conditions (including the conditions of a state health service) affect his reactions.

The psychoanalytic community and support of the Identity of the psychoanalyst. Why do psychoanalytic societies have such an intense scientific life when truly original contributions remain quite rare? One of the reasons seems to be that scientific communications in a psychoanalytic society seem to have not only the purpose of training and informing but also of reassuring the group and each member individually about his psychoanalytic identity. At a deeper level, to talk in different ways is to admit that the experience we talk about is a common one, that we can talk differently about the same things.

But is the identity of the psychoanalyst so closely linked with a narcissistic doubt? Or is it the consciousness which we form of this identity that is at stake? Widlöcher thinks the two are correlated. It is probably because at the level of our psychoanalytical activity our identity is threatened by the extensions of this practice that we feel the need to give ourselves a conscious representation of this activity. Discussion of our difficulties is essential in this. The study of our resistances and contradictions maintains an analytical process for the group.

* * *

These two papers, the abstracts of which appear above, are very different in orientation, but they represent two strains in psychoanalysis which have been present almost from the beginning. Though these strains are complementary, they are in some ways contradictory, and I do not think that Freud, or probably any of us, have quite succeeded in coming to terms with their relationship.

The first strain concerns the quest for a new experience of truth and the location of the psychoanalyst's position in this search. Probably the most common way in which psychoanalysts orientate themselves to the problem, and to my mind the least adequate, is to say that psychoanalysis is a science. It is certainly true that it grew out of and derived much of its theory from the physicalistic science of the nineteenth century. However, this imposes a rather arbitrary perspective on it because it has never been in any significant way experimental and has never produced covering laws capable of a high degree of proof or disproof. What seems to me to be the most important aspect of the claim of psychoanalysis to be a science is the passionate desire that it represents to affirm that new truths about the human psyche have been discovered by revolutionary modes of observation of process, giving rise to new and startling interpretations of it. In fact these interpretations are mostly historical in nature, and to reach them psychoanalysts use what rigor of logic they can—as do, for instance, jurists or literary critics. When applied to individuals, they are in general complex acts of assessment with a loose and variable relationship to covering law. Indeed to decide what covering law to apply may itself be a matter of complex assessment.

The importance of this is that it gives to psychoanalysis a very strong contemplative slant. And as its conclusions emphasize the early origin, continuity, and structuralization of modes of psychic reaction, its view of life can best be summarized, to borrow S. E. Hyman's word, as tragic. It is in order to convey the experience of the tragic that psychoanalysts, as Widlöcher emphasizes, have always stressed the central importance of the training analysis as a mode of passing on the essence of psychoanalysis. Though the experience of the training analysis may be a technical necessity in enabling analysts to know what to do when confronted with a patient, Widlöcher, in my opinion rightly, stresses the centrality of the encounter. This is where the mystery takes place, in which one human understands another, and the sense of wonder is engendered at the persistence of unconscious patterns without which no psychoanalyst can feel at home in his profession.

The strain which lies in not entirely easy conjunction with this is the strain which responds to the pressure for therapy and even cure. Psychoanalysis, like other therapies of psychological disorders, grew out of the demand for rationally based treatment as the power of religion to contain chronic suffering diminished after the Enlightenment. The present-day pressures are enormous; therapies proliferate to meet infinitely expanding need. Philip Rieff designated this situation "the triumph of the therapeutic." In this triumph psychoanalysts, by virtue of a more tragic orientation, may exercise a restraining hand.

Freud was a scientist (whose hobby was archaeology) fascinated by the nature and evolution of organic life. He was not by nature a therapist but became one in response to economic and social pressures. Although therapeutically he was on the whole very cautious, he oscillated (I believe) between his tragic view of the neuroses as severe constitutional defects from which the therapeutic results of analysis were a bonus wrested with great difficulty and an inevitable inclination toward therapeutic overoptimism, in which he thought, for example, that the results of analysis gave protection for life. Some of this oscillation is traced in Strachey's editorial note on "Analysis Terminable and Interminable" (1964). His optimism may also perhaps be illustrated (for example) by his footnote in 1923 to the Rat Man case history of 1909 (Freud 1909, p. 249) in which he claims that the patient's mental health was restored to him.

I would now like to refer briefly to the way in which the two papers which have been summarized illustrate these two aspects of psychoanalytic thinking—the endopsychic, tragic, and perhaps in a general sense religious outlook, and the outlook which rightly and necessarily struggles with the pressing problem of accommodating our thought and practice to a rapidly changing society. I will then outline some difficulties that I think play a part in the crisis of identity, or perhaps failure of nerve, or corruption by success, which besets us. I will then suggest some topics which seem to emerge from the two papers.

Widlöcher is not sure that there is a crisis, and he does not really believe that we are concerned with our identity. He thinks that our picture of ourselves (*la conscience que nous nous formons de notre identité*) is uncertain because we are molding our evolution. He puts forward the hypothesis (as does Joseph) that this confusion arises just because we have become integrated with the culture. What he does know is that we can't rely on our identification with Freud any longer. This I believe to be a crucial point, and I will come back to it. His own definition of the psychoanalytic identity is operational: it is defined by what the psychoanalyst understands and what he does. And the essence of his understanding and confidence in himself comes from the psychoanalytic encounter. This is an endopsychic definition of identity. It is based on the enhancement of the analyst's sense of his reality as a person. It is from this basic standpoint that he discusses social problems. The sometimes frenetic scientific life of the psychoanalytical society is aimed as much at reminding psychoanalysts of their common experience of the psychoanalytic encounter as at discovery.

Joseph's approach to the problem of the psychoanalyst's identity also emphasizes the central importance of the training experience. But the way in which he considers the concept of identity from a developmental point of view, in which the individual gradually incorporates more and more identifications into his image of himself makes it clear that it is primarily of a different sort of identity that he speaks. If Widlöcher's concept is reminiscent of Puritanism, with its belief that salvation can be derived only from the crucial experience of Grace, then Joseph's concept recognizes the importance of good works. In more practical terms he tries to come to grips with enormous dangers of dilution and looks to the fostering of a series of steadily integrated identifications to check it: the development of scientific objectivity and flexibility, held together by membership of a pioneering branch of a healing profession, by medical responsibility and by affective bonds with a great leader, with teachers and colleagues. I agree that what he describes is of essential importance and that identifications play an immense role in enabling us to function practically and morally. But there is another aspect to this. He includes in his description some very dreary psychoanalysts, who clearly depress him as much as they do me, though we cannot fail to recognize them. In spite of their flexibility and scientific training, most of them, according to his description, "regard themselves primarily as therapists. The nature of the theory . . . is accepted as being well established, not subject to much change or alteration, having the quality of immutability and representing scientific truth." In other words, as dead. The investigative use of psychoanalysis, he says, has been regarded as the province of the very few. I agree with Widlöcher that all that glitters in a psychoanalytical society is not great science and would add that we cannot expect it to be. We are—at least in the larger societies—in a period of reconsideration and do not know where the next advance will come. Nonetheless I also consider that there is a certain stultification of psychoanalytic thought and would like to make some suggestions concerning some of its causes.

Perhaps a hint of the trouble comes in Joseph's paper when he emphasizes all those identifications. An identification means etymologically becoming the same as someone else. With all those identifications to go through, when is the poor psychoanalyst going to be himself? What does he need them all for? What is the danger against which he needs so much support? And is there a connection with the fact noted by Widlöcher that the psychic work demanded of the analyst, which along with his analysis lays the foundation of his identity—note the difference between identity and identification—is surrounded by a peculiar silence?

I think that Widlöcher opens up the central issue when he speaks of the enticements of the analysis, the fascination of the patient's world, the transference holds, and the analyst's difficulty in maintaining a specific method of mental functioning which does not come naturally to him. The essence of the analytical relationship from the analyst's side is that he must replace his desire to form an object relationship with a tendency to form an identification, or rather that he must form an object relationship of a very aim-inhibited kind with his ego while opening himself emotionally and instinctually to the patient's stimulation. In this way he first achieves the type of superficial and transitory identification known as empathy, but this is not enough. He must then hold the identification inside him, scrutinizing it both sympathetically and critically, that is to say, with just the right degree of ambivalence. All this he must do sitting behind the couch, that is, cut off from the normal cues of human responsiveness which dominate our relationships from suckling on, eye to eye, ego to ego. Although most of his patients are personable, youngish people who stimulate him by their appearance, the stories they tell, their voices, and their smell, he must hold himself in control, responding humanely, it is true, but always within the context of his professional role. And practically no word ever appears in the literature about how the analyst manages to form relationship after relationship of the most intimate kind with patient after patient, of the mourning that he must feel for each one of them, and of how he discharges it.

The analyst's emotional task is always immensely difficult. Coupled to it at the beginning of his career is the exacting intellectual task, not so much of making new observations (which can wait), as of finding a notation for his observations which will unite them into a theme and enable him to give an accurate and more or less spontaneous interpretation. I believe that it took me a good ten years of full-time psychoanalytic practice to feel myself a psychoanalyst and be able to accept patients without some degree of guilt and anxiety, and I know that I am not alone in this. The newly qualified analyst is, therefore, confronted with something which might be described as an ego loss. He needs support, and here he turns to various teachers, but primarily he turns to his identification with the analyst inside him who functions partly by means of a creative identification and partly as an ambivalently cathected introject, so that he may find himself on occasion repeating irrelevant interpretations to his patients twenty years later. For many years the younger psychoanalyst functions—or at any rate I functioned—in part with an analytical false self. In some measure perhaps even with an analytical false self struggling with a dying language, since Freud's language, though a superb and still necessary construction, is his language, and to combine discipleship with originality is a very hard task, as Nietzsche emphasized. (In Freud's own words, in a letter to Eva Rosenfeld quoted by Roazen [1975], "the goody-goodys are no good, and the naughty ones go away.") This process of identification and introjection must have started with Freud's pupils and been continued with particular strength in respect of other great teachers. Perhaps our stultification of thought comes partly from the fact that, along the lines that Freud described in his paper "On Transience" and again in "Mourning and Melancholia," we have never been able to come to terms with his

death—nor, as a consequence, to assess the measure of transience which his ideas must share with all other scientific,
philosophical, or religious ideas. This may lead to psychoanalytic rigidity and lifelessness, or to revolt. We are tempted
to preserve Freudian ideas in desiccated form, scotomatizing
the richness of human modes of experience. It is partly
because of the gradual realization that we do this, in which
we have been helped by the originality of several outstanding
personalities, that we can no longer rely on our identification
with Freud.

The central problem of psychoanalytical identity therefore
seems to me to lie in finding a balance between the years of
training necessary for a student often approaching mid-life or
past it to master a highly exacting conceptual system and
technique and the stultification of originality by the weight of
its authority. To this personal and theoretical dependency
should be added the effect of the economic sanctions which
are never wholly forgotten where analysts are dependent on
private practice for their livelihood, though these are seldom
mentioned. It is certainly in part for economic reasons that it
is so difficult to persuade psychoanalysts to talk as publicly
about their difficulties, as on the whole, they do when they
are candidates.

The effect of economic sanctions can be reduced by state
subvention. But state subvention (with other social changes)
seems often to have abetted the worldwide disappearance of
the full-time psychoanalyst. The cause of economic and social
justice favors the distribution of the benefits of applied
psychoanalysis as a human right and professors and often
hospital consultants who are employed by the state are
restricted in their ability to undertake long analyses. But the
cause of psychoanalysis demands the recognition of the length
of time that human development takes—for the patient and

for the analyst—and the toleration of apparent therapeutic failures which may prove to be considerable successes in terms of the patient's inner life and even bring direct therapeutic rewards after many years. If this kind of psycho-analysis is to continue, as in my opinion it must for the philosophical and scientific well-being of the analyst, then it may have to be financed in some countries by private patients who are by no means affluent. This means that its practitioners will have to face a lower standard of living than has been accorded to them in the past as medical or para-medical specialists. Perhaps their remuneration will be nearer to that now accorded to teachers and social workers. This may mean a decline in the number of doctors who apply for training. But a psychoanalysis more able to consider man's tragic nature would survive to balance mass therapeutics and perhaps be more widely available.

To conclude this section, I think that the sense of identity of the psychoanalyst depends essentially on one thing: an experience of conversion. By this I do not mean an intellectual conversion, but a change of mind and heart, a *metanoia*. This comes through understanding, through what Widlöcher calls an encounter. Perhaps this will be with a book or books in adolescence, deepened by the experience of analysis. It does not depend on subscribing with any undue suspension of disbelief to complex hypotheses. Therefore, provided the basic experience is sufficiently reinforced by practice, it does not matter what the psychoanalyst does in addition to formal analysis. The identity of the psychoanalyst depends on the analytic fire in his belly. But becoming an analyst who can respond as both an analyst and a person is a very long process. This is the challenge from psychoanalysis itself which every analyst has to meet, and the fire can go out of his belly.

If it does, it may be a personal crisis in identity, but it does not constitute a crisis of identity for psychoanalysis unless it becomes a general phenomenon. The question is whether it has done so. I think there are three areas of possible crisis.

First, there may be a crisis within the feelings of the psychoanalyst. Psychoanalytic ideas have stood the test of time well, but the psychoanalyst is no longer a pioneer. On the contrary, he may feel himself a prisoner. It is sometimes said that there have been few important new concepts for twenty years. This is not long in the history of science, and it does not take account of a considerable change of atmosphere in some societies, but it seems to have left many psychoanalysts with the feeling that they will have no original contribution to make unless they turn to applied psychoanalysis. They lack the excitement of spirit which comes from collaboration with a great leader who is still alive or at least vividly remembered. In this respect, those closely influenced by such figures as Melanie Klein or Jacques Lacan are probably at an advantage, especially if they take note of an increasing reaction among analysts, as in society, against the type of adulation characteristic of a revolution but dangerous to it, which was naturally accorded to Freud. The first question concerning the feelings of the psychoanalyst is therefore: Can anyone remain purely a psychoanalytic therapist without the continued excitement of new discovery?

As theories are tested by time their inadequacy for the complexities of life are exposed. We hear the rumble of new ideas which must one day modify our theory and practice and be synthesized with it. If that were not so, then psychoanalytical ideas would be unique in history. Many questions present themselves here. Is it true that the classical psychoanalytic setup has been exhausted of its riches as is sometimes suggested? If it is not, how has it come about that Freud's discovery in free association of a revolutionary new mode of observing the whole fabric of human thought and feeling now yields so little? Will psychoanalysis be helped or harmed by its application to psychotherapeutic (or other) practice? What sort of psychotherapists will psychoanalysts make? Can psychoanalysis survive if it is used only for training? Does psychoanalysis as we have known it open the way to a new era in the history of man to be characterized by psychological discovery, or is it the product of a culture which is being superseded, as medieval monasticism was largely superseded by a predominantly pastoral orientation to religious life? I do not know how psychoanalysis will change. What I do feel sure about, however, is that, while we rightly emphasize the benefits of the encounter, we pay too little attention to those elements which may ultimately turn people away from it. "Every time you learn something, it feels as though you'd lost something," says Andrew Undershaft in Shaw's *Major Barbara*. I do not think that in estimating the holding power of analysis on the analyst we should undervalue man's need for illusion. It is by illusion as much as by truth that man lives. And the illusion of the omnipotence of psychoanalysis, by which too many psychoanalysts have lived, has been destroyed. Perhaps the illusion of omnipotence can now be found more easily in the triumph of the therapeutic.

Secondly, there may be an area of crisis within the psychoanalytical societies. Is the teaching too repressive of new ideas, or is it too diluted? Is it slanted against originality? What proportion of those who resign from a psychoanalytical society comes from the most disturbed section of the membership? Or from the most intelligent? Should the societies teach analytical psychotherapy, and, if so, what is it? How will they manage if they do? Are the candidates too old when they are selected? How many times a week are the patients to attend for analysis, and where are they to come from?

Thirdly, there may be a crisis in relation to society. We have lived in the West through a socioeconomic era which allowed analysis to become as much a way of life as a therapy for some members of the middle class. These times may have passed. In both the papers there are references to the acceptance of psychoanalytically based therapy by society at large, and in many countries there are analysts who wish to commit psychoanalysis to a social cause. But what of the many members of this younger generation—and not so young any more either—who regard the infinite expansion of the therapeutic as a bourgeois mirage, with analysis only the symptom of a sick society, not the remedy for it? Will society become increasingly disillusioned with the triumph of the therapeutic? And will analysis have to develop a new role as an instrument of social research and social policy? Or can it retain its remarkable status as the most satisfying intellectual approach and best therapy for problems of personal conflict which may be intractable?

REFERENCES

Freud, S. (1909). Notes upon a case of obsessional neurosis. *Standard Edition* 10:158-320.

——— (1916). On transcience. *Standard Edition* 14:305-307.

——— (1917). Mourning and melancholia. *Standard Edition* 14:243-258.

Roazen, P. (1975). *Freud and His Followers.* New York: Alfred A. Knopf.

Strachey, J. (1964). Editorial note on "Analysis terminable and interminable." *Standard Edition* 23:211-215.

On the Dual Use of Historical and Scientific Method in Psychoanalysis (1968)

Insofar as my clinical papers stress the personal and subjective aspects of the analytic encounter they are a reaction against the one-sided claim of psychoanalysis to be a science. This in no way invalidates the objectivity of psychoanalysis. It means that such general laws as it can state are able to bear psychological fruit only if constantly reexpressed in terms of the individual. The essay distinguishes some of the elements of historical and natural scientific method, and relates the need of psychoanalysis for both to the overdetermination of psychic phenomena. It is therefore also a plea for greater toleration of varieties of opinion.

* * *

The desire to emphasize the parity of method in psycho-analysis and in other sciences had both a logical justification and a justification in terms of a contemporary challenge in the first decades of the century. The combination in Freud's genius of a unique insight into the unconscious with an ability to systematize his findings into general laws capable of a considerable degree of verification made his discoveries a potential turning point for mankind. Freud was not merely the Copernicus of the mind, who had the intuition of genius; he was also the Kepler who through forty years formulated the laws of its working.

As natural science had arisen from the breakup of the medieval order, so psychoanalysis arose in response to the social changes of the nineteenth century—the increased ap-plication of scientific method and the diminished tolerance of physical and moral suffering. The inherent conflict between scientific and religious premises encouraged both doctors and patients to seek naturalistic explanations for phenomena which had previously been within the domain of the priest. According to Zilboorg (1941), Charcot reclassified as hysteria phenomena well known to the Inquisition, which had re-garded many of its signs as dramatic evidence of demoniacal possession. Freud was educated in advanced traditions of naturalism; he described Brücke's physicalistic teaching as the most important intellectual influence of his life. Nonethe-less, psychoanalysis met an immediate rejection from the medical profession, and it was imperative to emphasize the scientific basis for its conclusions and to repudiate the charge that it was "an old wives' psychology." Most of Freud's early adherents possessed little or no status as scientists and the prestige of the subject was impaired by the controversies which broke out. The high aspirations and sense of mission of the early psychoanalysts, combined with the frustration of having their vital knowledge ignored, sometimes led them to claim validity for their method at the expense of a full admission of its difficulties. For instance, the claim that the psychoanalytic method is "the logical equivalent of the experimental method" leaves a certain sense of unreality. Psychoanalysis is primarily a method of clinical investigation. It is difficult to believe that the pressures towards action involved in caring for acutely ill people do not sometimes render the comparison with experimental science inappropriate. Miller (1966) has deprecated such a comparison for medicine. In any event the comparison accords insufficiently with the experience of discussions with colleagues, even of similar theoretical viewpoint, let alone with the recurrent division of psychoanalysts into acrimoniously disputing schools. Though controversy has always beset science, the division into schools clearly marks some degree of failure in the power to apply the experimental method. How often can we really say, as Waelder did in 1939, that the work of the psychoanalyst should be compared with that of the detective, the gradual accumulation of clues leading to one inevitable conclusion? In fairness to Waelder, he admitted at the time that this was a tall order, but thought his description correct in principle. Twenty years later his approach to the problem was more modest (Waelder 1962).

It is true that psychoanalysts may maintain that scientific method is based on broader concepts than a combination of measurement and prediction, and that this view is supported by philosophers of science, and probably by most scientists working in experimental fields. The recognition of the broad base of a scientific method does not imply, however, that its difficulties should not be fully explored. Some of these may be illustrated from the symposia on validation of the American Psychoanalytical Association in 1955, when Brenner listed a series of responses which might be taken to indicate that an interpretation was correct. The first three were: a diminution of anxiety; symptomatic improvement, or its opposite in a case where there is a predominant need to suffer; and a confirmatory memory, fantasy, dream, or other verbal association, or a confirmatory gesture, all of them with or without an appropriate emotional experience. Any of these events can be experienced by analyst and patient alike as convincing confirmation, but it is evident that this by itself would leave the problem both too loosely and too narrowly conceived. The intrinsic relationship of the response to the interpretation remains indeterminate. This is particularly clear when Brenner gives equal, or even preferential status to a diminution of anxiety as a response, compared with a confirmatory memory or dream. As Eleanor Steele pointed out (1955), there are too many indefinable "hitchhikers" with each interpretation for it to be judged solely by its ostensible intellectual content. I would add that even the intellectual content of an interpretation and its "confirmation" may not always be easy to define.

The differences between an interpretation and a typical scientific hypothesis will be discussed in more detail later. But there is also a wider problem: the "correctness" of an interpretation cannot be assessed in isolation from the fit of the analysis as a whole to the total personality. The "correctness" of interpretations are most satisfactorily evaluated only when patient and analyst alike have gained distance from the analysis. Freud never wrote a case history until the treatment was ended. His caution is reflected in his admission in the "Dora" case that as time passed. he realized that his interpretations had failed to take adequate account of her latent homosexuality and of the transference.

The difficulties of the scientific methodology of psychoanalysis are clearly illustrated by the fact that the evidential problems leading to division into schools have not been better defined. At best the controversies have tended to center on the question of what assumptions may be considered to be logically permissible. The question of how some psychoanalysts can find confirmation for their interpretations which others repudiate as unconvincing has been largely ignored as a methodological problem. As usual, Freud came nearest to the heart of the matter when he gave his opinion that the main difficulty was contained in the old saying *"Quot capita, tot sensus"*—"as many heads, so many opinions." It is a thesis of this paper that the tendency to partisanship is fostered by considering psychoanalytic methodology exclusively in terms of scientific methodology. Since the historical method is near to the soil of the clinical method, discussion may sometimes be more profitably furthered by considering psychoanalysis from the standpoint of historical method.

That the genetic approach in psychoanalysis may be compared with that of the historian has been widely recognized. In spite of exceptions, however, reference to the writings of methodologists of history plays a comparatively small role in discussions of the methodology of psychoanalysis. For instance, in the American symposia on validation, the limitations of the scientific viewpoint in psychoanalysis were stressed by several speakers, but there is no report of a speaker who stressed the advantages of comparing psychoanalysis with history.

Hartmann has considered the relationship of the two methods. While appreciating the value of Dilthey's (1924) distinction between understanding and explanation, he has emphasized (1927) that "many understandable connections ... are ... actually causal connections" and concluded (1959) that while psychoanalysts study the individual's "life-history," "it would be misleading . . . to classify this aspect of analysis as a historical discipline. . . ". Concern with developmental problems "should not obfuscate the fact that the aim of these studies is . . . to develop law-like propositions." At the 24th International Psycho-Analytical Congress in 1965 he suggested that the historical aspects of the method had been overstressed.

Philosophers, professionally sensitive to distinctions among types of explanation, have sometimes accorded a greater importance to the historical approach. Flew (1956) concluded that "the fundamental concepts of psychoanalysis . . . are precisely the notions which rational agents employ to give account of their own conduct," and that this makes psychoanalysis

> a peculiarly rational enterprise, though in a sense which makes this assertion quite compatible with a claim that the methods of analysis are unscientific; that . . . it would be a mistake to attempt a logical reduction of these notions to physicalistic terms;

and, finally, that

> comparisons between psychoanalysis and other disciplines dealing with men and their motives—history for example—might help to illuminate some of the dark places of the former.

Meyerhoff (1964) drew attention to the role of subjective elements in history and in psychoanalysis, and to the fruitful interaction on one another of historical and scientific methods. Among psychoanalysts, Erikson (1958) seems to be unusual in referring, as does Meyerhoff, to Collingwood, whose elaboration of the thought of Croce provided the outstanding influence in the English-speaking world of the last half century on the methodology of history. He quotes sympathetically Collingwood's (1946) definition of a historical process as one "in which the past, so far as it is historically known, survives in the present," as relevant at least to the self-conscious activity of the clinician. Home (1966) criticized the claims of psychoanalysis to be a science. While Home appreciated the epistemological significance of understanding by identification, as opposed to explanation, he made a more questionable distinction between scientific thought, concerned with facts, and that of the humanities (such as psychoanalysis) concerned with interpretation. My own view is similar to that of Meyerhoff. Both methods are used fruitfully. But I think that a great deal of confusion remains, leading to an overestimation of our powers of explanation, thanks to a failure to differentiate their functions in greater detail. To attempt such a differentiation is the main aim of this paper.

The existence of varying schools of thought is of course no sign in itself that a subject is not justly classed as a science. The history of all sciences has been beset by controversies. Interpretation in science almost regularly becomes subject to controversy, when access to experiment cannot be achieved, or when an attempt is being made to unify theory. Scientists have often used intuitive methods to arrive at their theories, as is now well known. But what distinguishes the aim of scientific method, and usually the calibre of the great scientist, is the ability to devise acceptable methods for testing hypotheses which may themselves have been reached by intuition or by logic alone. This is what the divines at the Council of Trent (1545–1563 A.D.) understood as crucial, according to Whitehead, when they objected to the empiricism of the scientists as a devaluation of reason.

To maintain that there is a distinction between historical and scientific method is in itself controversial, though there can be little difficulty in agreeing that the testing of historical propositions is a more problematical procedure than the testing of hypotheses in an experimental science. The essence of history has been considered to lie in its capacity to provide explanations, and Langlois and Seignobos, for instance, have said (1898) "L'histoire, éxplicative avant tout, mérite bien le nom de science." Bury (1903) similarly gave his opinion "History . . . is simply a science, no less and no more." In recent times, Popper (1957), in spite of his antipathy to determinism, has maintained that explanations of the past are in logical form no different from predictions.

Among the Greeks there was certainly no distinction between natural science and history. The word *historia* means inquiry, and Herodotus, the earliest known historiographer (as opposed to chronicler) was strongly under the influence of the medical school of Hippocrates, just as the German historians of the nineteenth century, exemplified by Mommsen, sought to emulate the methods of the scientists of the nineteenth century. It was the aim of Herodotus to look into past events in order to replace *doxa* by *episteme*, opinion by knowledge, and thus, by skillful questioning, to perform a task which, according to Collingwood, the Greeks had thought impossible.

However, a distinction between two paths to knowledge became acute with the emergence of experimental science at the Renaissance. In the Middle Ages, science had meant knowledge of any kind. In 1725 the word appeared in the English language with a meaning defined by the Oxford Dictionary as follows:

A branch of study which is concerned either with a connected body of demonstrated truths or with observed facts systematically classified and more or less colligated by being brought under general laws, and which includes trustworthy methods for the discovery of new truth within its own domain.

If we follow this definition, the view of the historian as a scientist can most plausibly be illustrated by the work of historians such as Buckle or Spengler, or the Marxist historians, who set out to describe the laws which govern the evolution of society. But not only is the type of historical generalization which is reached notoriously impermanent, but the work of the vast majority of historians in all ages has not been of this kind. In practice what historians mostly study is human thought and motive. This is similar to the main object of study of the psychoanalyst in his patient. The psychoanalyst's interest in the past is, of course, for the purpose of explaining the present, whereas this is much less directly true of the majority of historians.

If the reconstruction of past human thought is regarded as a science, then, as Collingwood noted, it is a science of a somewhat special kind, since the path of inference from anything that can be compared with observations is extremely indirect. Not one inferential step, but a chain of inference is usually required before the historian can begin to conceptualize the real object of study. Magna Carta is a legal document formulated from many precursors. What Magna Carta in fact meant for administrative and social relationships in the thirteenth century remains a more difficult question than the tracing of its derivation. Each clause requires a separate evaluation. But it has to be accepted that Magna Carta will not sustain a great many of the interpretations which it received in the seventeenth and in the nineteenth centuries. Reconstruction based on indirect chains of reasoning tends to receive varied formulation in the mind of each individual historian. Historians, and philosophers of history who have also been historians, have therefore often opposed the view that history is a science. Croce (1915, 1941), Collingwood (1946), Trevelyan (1913), and Butterfield (1931) are examples. The dispute over the essential nature of historical reasoning continues after a century. It is permissible to regard such a continuance of a philosophical controversy as a sign that it is in an insoluble phase.* It therefore seems appropriate to accept the view which Gardiner formulated in *The Nature of Historical Explanation* (1952). He emphasized that there is a "slide" from explanations of a scientific type in history, which are concerned with covering law, to those of "historical type proper." I should like to define the distinctions which I would make, and refer them to psychoanalysis.

The aim of science is ideally to provide unitary explanations of multiple phenomena. This is what is implied by the theory of covering law. A psychoanalytic science exists which is built up from covering laws, examples of which are the libido theory, or the theory of the interpretability of a range of clinical phenomena in terms of the theory of transference. A further example of a covering law is the law of psychic overdetermination, that is, (as I understand it) that there may be multiple motivation for a single phenomenon of psychic expression. But with the admission of the validity of the principle of overdetermination recognition is achieved that the psychoanalyst is forced to operate in many areas of his practice with a logical method which contrasts strongly with the usual method of science. Instead of finding unitary

---

*In spite of Berlin's opinion (1954) that since Popper's *Poverty of Historicism* there is no excuse for regarding history as a science.

explanations for multiple events, he must find multiple explanations for unitary events. The criterion of acceptability of an interpretation cannot in these circumstances be simply his success in elucidating a covering law, since, as Freud understood, explanations may have to be offered simultaneously on levels which are only loosely compatible with one another, and a single law uniting them is not to be defined. This mode of explanation is the antithesis of what would be required by Occam's razor.

The sense of conviction which can be derived from such explanations is, therefore, due not to the elucidation of a covering law but to the judgment that a complex assessment of the interrelationship of psychological motives and external pressures has been satisfactorily achieved. This is a judgment of process, rooted in the immediate or distant past of the individual, and as such a judgment of historical type. It is in fact a consequence of the multiplicity of explanations possible in history that every historian will emphasize the significance of different causal connections. Butterfield has pointed out in *The Whig Interpretation of History* (1931) that every historian in fact writes the history of his own generation. Freud said something analogous when he confessed that he tended to interpret his patients' material in terms of the problem which was interesting him at the time. All this can be summarized by saying that in psychoanalysis there is some degree of shift in the criteria of success in explanation from those of natural science, which center on objective criteria of verification determined by the material to be studied, to the criteria of historical interpretation which accord more weight to endopsychic satisfaction.

The psychoanalyst is confronted with his phenomena as a totality. The experimental scientist sets out to isolate each variable of the process to be studied in order to formulate a single hypothesis and test it. The prediction which he makes is typically on the basis of a single law. For the psychoanalyst, as for the historian in Gardiner's description of his work, to understand the phenomena in terms of a single law is only one problem among several. What also concerns him is to know which law to apply at a given moment, and how the laws may be considered to interact. It is true that the psychoanalyst attempts to group phenomena, and therefore in a sense to isolate them, by an assessment of similarities conveyed to the patient in the form of an interpretation. Here again however he acts more like a historian who interprets a developing process. When the psychoanalyst's assessment is shared by the patient at a preconscious level of ego-functioning the result is that the phenomenology of the analysis is "clarified." The patient brings an increasing number of associations which will accord with the same explanation, so that the explanation itself deepens in its complexity and range of applicability to past and present events. This process is highly satisfying to patient and analyst alike, and seems to have some relationship with therapeutic success. As a psychoanalyst, in the course of his development, acquires increasing skill in clarifying his patient's material in this way, so he acquires an increasing confidence in his power to help a broader spectrum of his patients, as well as a greater ease in his work. But this is a very different type of selection from that made by a scientist in an experiment. It is a sign that a certain accord has been reached between the observer and the patient who is observed, at least for the duration of that part of the analysis. This accord and interaction take place in the context of an intense love relationship on the part of the observed for the observer, imposing an admitted strain on the objectivity and ease of functioning of the observer.

The extent to which the observations of the scientists themselves impose distortion or variation on the facts to be isolated and studied has been prominent in scientific thinking at least since Whitehead's *Adventures of Ideas* (1926). It may be doubted if the emotional stimulation of the observer by his observational data is often as intense, or of the same order as in psychoanalysis. That such an emotional potential exists is recognized in the discussions of the ramifications of what are usually classed as transference and countertransference phenomena, and to some extent regarded as pathological. What the literature does not stress is the immense impact of the value system of patient and analyst alike on the interpretations which are given, and the total analysis that results. But it emerges in every second analysis of a patient by a new analyst that the alteration in the manner and matter of each analyst's understanding, according to the differing ethos of each, is profound. Even the divisions between schools may depend upon classes of value system as well as on controversies over the significance of evidence.

The psychoanalyst's valuations are, like the historian's, for the most part orientated to the patient's past. In "Der Begriff der Deutung in der Psychoanalyse" (1932) ("The Concept of Interpretation in Psychoanalysis") Bernfeld maintained that a reconstruction of past events is not a reconstruction of the patient's motivation *(Absicht),* though the whole of psychoanalytic interpretation for any individual hinges on the question of motivation. Though most psychoanalysts would lose confidence if a correlation with actual events were not supplied by the patient with some constancy, psychoanalytic reconstructions are essentially aimed at psychic experience. In spite of dramatic successes, such as that revealed by Marie Bonaparte's confirmation (1939), on the basis of the *Cinq Cahiers,* of Freud's reconstruction of her observations of her nurse's intercourse and its effects, the relationship between reconstruction of events and of intention in practice remains variable. Bernfeld concluded that the psychoanalyst does not so much reconstruct events as build a model of the personality. Before returning to the reasons for preferring to regard reconstruction as a historical rather than as a scientific technique, I should like to give two examples of the difficulty of the method. The first comes from history and illustrates the difficulty in reconstructing motivation when the reconstruction of the facts is unassailable; the second is from the psychoanalytic literature and refers to the difficulty in reconstructing the facts even when the motivation is understood.

In 1670 Charles II of England signed a treaty at Dover with Louis XIV. The financially harassed English king agreed to come to the help of France to overthrow the United Provinces of the Netherlands. Historians could reconstruct that a secret *quid pro quo* must have been agreed. In the present century the postulated Secret Treaty of Dover was discovered in a drawer of an old desk. In it Louis agreed to pay Charles a personal income of £200,000 a year in return for his agreement to lead England back to Catholicism. The reconstruction of events was conclusively confirmed, but the question of Charles II's motivation—whether he really intended to lead England back to Catholicism or merely to use Louis XIV to solve his financial problems—remained as enigmatical as before.

The second example is from the manner of Freud's reconstruction of the Wolf Man's observation of parental intercourse. The Wolf Man's sexual compulsions led Freud to conclude that observations or fantasies of the sexual intercourse of his parents had been decisive for his character formation. The importance of experiences and fantasies of parental intercourse for the formation of introjects is now

generally recognized, and this discovery is one of the outstanding examples of Freud's psychological genius. When
Freud's argument is examined in detail, however, one sees
that he does not explain all the steps in it with equal clarity. It
is easy to understand his assumption that the patient used
reversal as a defense in order to transform a scene of violent
movement into a scene of uncanny stillness. He does not
explain, however, why the patient abandoned the defense of
reversal in respect of his parents' white underclothes, the
color of which survives unchanged in the whiteness of the
wolves. The result is that whereas Freud's inference that the
Wolf Man's sexual habits were influenced by fantasies or,
more probably, by observations of sexual intercourse between his parents or between animals, is generally convincing, some doubt remains—which Freud may be thought to
have shared—of the validity of the details of the postulated
scene of parental intercourse and therefore of the details
postulated to determine the Wolf Man's sexual behavior.

These examples illustrate two points concerning the use of
scientific principles in making reconstructions. When they
are aptly applied, as in the historical example, the problem of
motivation may remain. Even when the problem of motivation has been grasped, the technique of reconstruction of
detail may be too complex to be consistently applicable, as
Freud pointed out in "From the History of an Infantile
Neurosis" (1918) and in "Constructions in Analysis" (1937).
These uncertainties, as Bernfeld saw, imply that psychoanalysis shares all the difficulties of retrospective studies, of
which history is the prototype for human affairs.

The ultimate problem of knowledge for the psychoanalyst
is thus the same as for the historian: it consists in the special
requirement for each that he must recreate the psychic life of

his object of study within his own mind. History and psychoanalysis depend upon a process of identification. This contrasts with the work of the natural scientist, for whom
identification with nature and its laws is impossible, since
they are not subject to introspective awareness. It is this
difference, adumbrated by Dilthey's distinction between
understanding and explaining, which led Croce, Oakeshott
(1933) and Collingwood to formulate a principle summed up
in Collingwood's famous paradox, "All history is contemporary history," since the past can be studied only insofar as it
takes place currently in the mind of the historian. This is the
basis of Collingwood's assertion that the epistemological
position of historical studies is unique. Collingwood's position led to exaggeration. He maintained, for instance, that
when the historian understands Nelson's tactical motives at
the battle of Trafalgar his thought is identical with Nelson's.
Such a proposition raises difficult issues of the definition of
thought, and the relationship of conscious thought to its
unconscious substrate, and to the body. But it remains a great
advance in philosophical insight to perceive that an act of
intuition by identification with the thoughts and feelings of
another human being is a creative act which deserves to be
distinguished in type from an act of creative intuition which
does not depend upon identification. In the first, the sources
of knowledge are weighted towards the revival in the historian or the psychoanalyst of endopsychic experience; in the
second, they are weighted towards testing reality in the
external world.

It has often been maintained by psychoanalysts that the
patient "relives" his past in the transference and thus trans-
forms the subject matter of history into an observational
study in the present. It is necessary to consider what is meant

by such phrases as "repetition in the transference." Clearly, the phrase is not a description, but a metaphor; experiences cannot be repeated in a literal sense.* They cannot be "repeated" in any sense if they have not remained in some degree active in the patient's mind up to the time of the "repetition." What happens with the initiation of psychoanalytic therapy is that the relationship of the repressed memories to the ego's defenses is altered. Recathected by the desire for introspection and understanding in order to overcome frustration, the repressed memories now strive towards recall within the psychoanalytic session. The first stage of such recall, owing to the difficulty of modifying unconscious drives, tends to be the expression of an emotional attitude or piece of behavior directed towards the analyst. The metapsychological structure of the psychoanalytic session thus in some respects resembles the structure of a dream. Memories are cathected by unsatisfied desires and expressed in distorted form as words and behavior, just as in dreams they are expressed in distorted form as hallucinations.

But the same difficulties apply to the interpretation of these phenomena as to all other forms of reconstruction. It is not a matter of the simple "repetition" of a total experience, but of the recathexis of discrete aspects of memory under the impact of the desire for understanding within a particular context of interpretation. Indeed, it seems doubtful if the recall in the context of analytic support and adult mentation of even an affective reaction can be identical with the affective reaction of a child.

*It may seem unnecessary to labor this point when Heraclitus emphasized more than two thousand years ago that no man steps into the same river twice. But it seems to me that Heraclitus is often forgotten in psychoanalytic discussion.

Not infrequently an interpretation can be convincingly supported. But the return to consciousness of an affect-laden memory is not to be confused with repetition. The "compulsion to repeat" in the transference refers rather to attitudes, reactions, symptomatic acts. As such they are already phenomena which may be more discretely formulated than the repressed memories to which they allude. For instance, falling off a swing may have to be represented by stumbling at the door of the consulting room. This is again not a matter of simple repetition, but of the formation *de novo* of a symptomatic act designed to give expression to a repressed memory in a form suitable to the physical conditions of analysis. Such symptomatic acts are often more restricted in their reference to past events than were the complex attitudes which we suppose as their precursors. The attitude to the analyst of the adult patient who stumbles at the door cannot be identical with her attitude as a child to the sister who "by accident on purpose" pushed her off the swing. The same difficulties apply to the interpretation of affective patterns as to all other forms of reconstruction. So far from being a matter of simple repetition, it is a question of the expression of psychic formations designed, in varying degrees, both to represent and screen elements of a total experience.

In contrast to this, a view of reconstruction in analysis is sometimes maintained which accords to it a very high scientific status as "a prediction into the past," confirmed by the patient's subsequent memories or associations. Even if this view were accepted, both the prediction and its confirmation are of a different order from the type of prediction which is the hallmark of the natural sciences. As has been emphasized, scientific prediction is typically based on the operation of a single law. The weakness of Popper's argument that assumptions about human behavior must be made in order to obtain agreement on the likelihood of historical reconstructions is immediately apparent. Whereas the scientist who designs an experiment to test a hypothesis knows exactly what his hypothesis is, the historian's hypotheses, as Gardiner emphasizes, are implicit and extremely difficult, if not impossible, to define.

Sometimes psychoanalytic reconstructions may, of course, be simple in structure, and be conclusively confirmed by memories. But Freud pointed out in his paper on "Constructions in Analysis" (1937) that what in general differentiates reconstructions from interpretations is that interpretation applies to a single element, whereas reconstructions concern "a piece of" the patient's "early history which he has forgotten." Since only a part of the total can normally be constructed at any time, the patient's response—for instance his refusal to accept an apparently valid reconstruction—may be based on unconscious knowledge of modifying factors. This situation is again very similar to that in history. Namier's clarification (1929) from confidential papers of the nature of parliamentary groupings in the reign of George III, or Maitland's elucidation (1898) of a point of Canon law from the procedure for burning a heretic (a deacon who turned Jew for love of a Jewess) still require to be understood within a wider attempt to reconstruct the psychology of an age. The analogy between psychoanalytic reconstruction and reconstruction in history is far closer than the analogy with prediction in natural science.

It would be wrong to feel certain, even at the end of a long analysis, that the model of the personality achieved could not be subjected to modification. The psychological processes are of great complexity, and their interrelationships capable of being differently interpreted. Such phrases as "the patient relives his past in the transference" are crude expressions which telescope the psychic processes. In the course of development the drives become increasingly bound with cathexes of object representations, and modes of defense become habitual, so that psychic life inevitably bears a certain stamp of repetition. But the reconstruction of the psychic life of the child in psychoanalysis is inevitably partial and can only be loosely compared with prediction from a scientific law.

Prediction is also said to be used to foretell the emerging layers of the patient's associations. Here again the same objections apply: the theme of the patient's associations is capable of very variable assessment. Besides, experienced analysts differ in their view of the extent to which the smooth and logical development of the material is an artifact imposed by the technique of selection for interpretation. In any case the power of "prediction" functions with great variability; it is insufficient to prevent periods of puzzlement in every analysis. To what extent an analyst can in fact foretell the course of psychoanalytic material will be difficult to estimate as long as we have almost exclusively retrospective studies at our disposal. Only the recording of assessments made at the time can test their reliability as predictions, as Kris emphasized. The evidence which the psychoanalyst can use in such studies is at present based on inexact observation-records, distorted by secondary revision. His ability to convince his readers is proportional either to the complexity of logical relationship which he can bestow on the phenomena, or to the well-argued originality (or unoriginality) of his views. His account carries conviction by the same criteria as are applied to a work of history, to legal argument, or to philosophy or literary criticism. Truth therefore becomes in some degree a function of the number of judges, since the individual evaluations of an account of a psychoanalytic treatment seem always to remain variable.

It is in considering psychoanalytic controversies that the advantages of emphasizing the value of an historical orientation are greatest. The inherent value of the historical method is that controversies between psychoanalysts will be interpreted with regard to their meaning as historical phenomena, and not simply as technical disputes in a technical discipline. When he considered the secession from psychoanalysis of Freud's Swiss collaborators, Jones drew attention (1955) not merely to the personal and intrapsychic factors involved, but also to general considerations of the influences on the formation of the Swiss character of the peculiarities of Swiss history. In doing so he set a welcome example. Today it is easier to understand the secession of both Jung and Adler as in part determined by the lack at the time of an ego psychology, which left them confronted with the unconscious in a way which was too difficult for them to assimilate. The lack of an ego psychology itself had historical determinants, in the magnitude of Freud's discovery of the dynamic unconscious and possibly in its appeal as a revolt against the naive materialism of the physicalistic tradition, and an oppressive sexual morality. Similarly, it may be possible to understand the increasing preoccupation with the theory of the death instinct, not merely as an attempt at an epistemological solution of a problem in psychoanalytic theory, but also as the result of the impact on Freud and other analysts of their confrontation with human aggression in the first World War. To place psychoanalytic theories in a historical context follows a mode of explanation which has been applied to other sciences impressively, for instance, by Clark in *The Seventeenth Century* (1947).

In regard to later controversies, not only the theories themselves need to be assessed, but the impact on the weltanschauung of analysts of migrations, or of a change of focus of interest when a sexual revolution, in which an earlier generation of analysts had been pioneers, has largely been won. We should not only accord a high valuation to the historical method in discussing the psychoanalytic method; it is also of value for assessing the significance of our controversies and our difficulties with the world and with each other.

REFERENCES

Berlin, I. (1954). *Historical Inevitability.* Auguste Comte Memorial Lecture. London: Oxford University Press.

Bernfeld, S. (1932). Der Begriff der Deutung in der Psychoanalyse. *Zeitschrift fur Angewandte Psychologie* 42:448–497.

Bonaparte, M. (1939). *Five Copy Books.* London: Imago, 1950–1953.

Brenner, C. (1955). Contribution to panel on validation of psychoanalytical techniques (J. Marmor, reporter). *Journal of the American Psychoanalytic Association* 3:496–505.

Bury, J. B. (1903). *The Science of History.* London: Cambridge University Press.

Butterfield, H. (1931). *The Whig Interpretation of History.* London: George Bell.

Clark, Sir George (1947). *The Seventeenth Century.* London: Oxford University Press.

Collingwood, R. G. (1946). *The Idea of History.* London: Oxford University Press.

Croce, B. (1915). *The Theory and History of Historiography.* London: Harrap, 1921.

—— (1941). *History as the Story of Liberty* trans. S. Sprigge. London: Allen & Unwin.

Dilthey, W. (1924). Ideen über eine beschreibende und zergliedernde Psychologie. *Gesammelte Schriften* 5. Leipzig: Teubner.

Erikson, E. H. (1958). The nature of clinical evidence. *Daedalus* 87 (4):65–87.

Flew, A. (1956). Motives and the unconscious. *Minnesota Studies in the Philosophy of Science,* Vol. 1. Minneapolis: University of Minnesota Press.

Freud, S. (1918). From the history of an infantile neurosis. *Standard Edition* 17.
––––– (1933). New Introductory Lectures. *Standard Edition* 22:3–182.
––––– (1937). Constructions in Analysis. *Standard Edition* 23:255–270.
Gardiner, P. (1952). *The Nature of Historical Explanation.* London: Oxford University Press.
Hartmann, H. (1927). Understanding and explanation. In *Essays on Ego Psychology.* London: Hogarth, 1964.
––––– (1959). Psychoanalysis as a scientific theory. In *Essays on Ego Psychology.* London: Hogarth, 1964.
Home, H. J. (1966). The concept of mind. *International Journal of Psycho-Analysis* 47:42–49.
Jones, E. (1955). *Sigmund Freud: His Life and Work,* vol 2. London: Hogarth.
Langlois, C. V. and Seignobos, C. (1898). *Introduction to the Study of History,* trans. G. G. Berry. London: Duckworth.
McKechnie. (1905) *Magna Carta: A Commentary on the Great Charter of King John.* London: Maclehose.
Maitland, F. W. (1898). *Roman Canon Law in the Church of England.* London: Methuen.
Meyerhoff, H. (1964). On psychoanalysis as history. In *Psychoanalysis and the Human Situation,* ed. U. Marmorston and E. Stainbrook, pp. 84–105. New York: Vantage Press.
Miller, H. (1966). Fifty years after Flexner. *Lancet* 2:647.
Namier, L. (1929). *The Structure of Politics at the Accession of George III.* London: Macmillan.
Oakeshott, M. (1933). *Experience and its Modes.* London: Cambridge University Press.
Popper, K. (1957). *The Poverty of Historicism.* London: Routledge & Kegan Paul.
Steele, E. (1955). Contribution to panel on validation of psychoanalytical techniques. *Journal of the American Psychoanalytic Association* 3.
Trevelyan, G. M. (1913). *Clio: A Muse and Other Essays.* London: Longmans Green.

Waelder, R. (1939). Kriterien der Deutung. *Internationale Zeitschrift für Psychoanalyse* 24:136–145.

—— (1962). Psychoanalysis, scientific method and philosophy. *Journal of the American Psychoanalytic Association* 10.

Whitehead (1926). *Science and the Modern World.* London: Cambridge University Press.

—— (1933). *Adventures of Ideas.* London: Cambridge University Press.

Zilboorg, G. (1941). *History of Medical Psychology.* New York: Norton.

APPENDIX B

The Psychical
Roots of Religion:
A Case Study
(1973)

Man's need for fantasy is nowhere so evident as in the high valuation placed on religion by the individual and society in all epochs—including perhaps our own epoch of messianic socialism. Religion characteristically asserts that something incredible not only compels belief but a belief that is necessary to salvation. It does so in order to express man's unconscious knowledge that his psychological strength comes from having survived incredible experiences in childhood which he can no longer recapture except through symbolism.

Psychoanalysis also derives its power to strengthen by reviving incredible early experiences, and by revealing the truth behind nonsense; but it must be careful not to share the dogmatism of Western religion.

*   *   *

Freud's genius lay in his understanding of the importance of fantasy formation for the fate of the individual. But his grasp of its importance for society in terms of the mythopoetic function of religion was much weaker.

In the least convincing strand in Freud's writings on religion he saw it as "patently infantile" and "the obsessional neurosis of mankind." However, he became dissatisfied with his failure in The Future of an Illusion (1927) to account for the high value set on religion by the individual and by society, and tried to remedy it in Civilization and its Discontents (1930) by suggesting that the glory of God might have its psychical roots in the child's impressions of the power of his father. He confessed himself puzzled by the psychical roots of the great mother deities who seemed everywhere to have preceded the father gods. The most satisfactory strand in Freud's views on religion was his recognition of the importance of myth for the transmission of culture. This was expounded particularly in his last work, Moses and Monotheism (1939), but his whole theory of society (Totem and Taboo, 1913) was a modern version of the theory of the social contract making religion its cement. The psychical roots of Christianity, the religion which has dominated our culture for sixteen centuries, Freud virtually ignored; and in spite of notable exceptions, such as Erich Fromm (1963) and Theodor Reik (1958), most psychoanalysts have done the same since.

The importance of religion as a cement of society seems to be illustrated by the high social status conceded to religious organizations and leaders—at least until recently. And religious faith has often been counted as a criterion of the reliability and cohesion of an individual's character. Since the intelligence of a child of five may be sufficient to expose the logical weakness of a religious myth, as Freud showed in the Wolf Man story (1918), some explanation of the value placed on religion is clearly required. In this connection Arlow (1961) has emphasized the power of the instinctual wish expressed in the myth to attract identification with the hero in the ego.

In attempting the beginnings of my own explanation I shall start with a description of faith given by a famous convert to religious belief. Leo Tolstoy described faith as "the force whereby we live"—"that sense by virtue of which man does not destroy himself, but continues to live on."

This description of faith does not refer, however, to belief in any religious myth or formulation. It refers to the inner consciousness of a force that, whatever its origins, is now experienced as acting from within. It may, I think, be translated into psychoanalytical terms as the force which ensures that the individual will withstand instinctual frustration and tolerate tension between ego and ego-ideal without the danger of a murderous attack upon the ego by the superego. Or, put another way, it is the faith in the indestructibility of good internalized objects.

But why in religion must an inner conviction be sustained by a belief in a series of external events of a highly improbable kind? Or even, one might think, of an incredible kind? Is it because the experiences on which the conviction is based are beyond the recall of consciousness and can therefore be expressed only by allusions or symbols? For the psychological facts are surely as Tolstoy portrayed them in his description of the priest in *Resurrection* (1903) who added an extra service for the convicts out of the goodness of his heart: "He did not believe that the bread turned into flesh . . . or that he had actually swallowed a bit of God. No one could believe this; but he believed that one ought to believe it." Why do people believe that they ought to believe the incredible? Perhaps the answer will come more easily if the question is reframed. Why does the symbolic nature of the religious myth have to be denied, and the myth instead asserted to be literally true? From what emotional source does the argument *"Credo quia impossibile"* ("I believe it *because* it is impossible") derive its strength? Freud showed in *The Interpretation of Dreams* (1900) that the sense of reality in a dream indicates that a real experience of importance at present outside consciousness is being alluded to, and he illustrated the point in "Delusions and Dreams in Jensen's *Gradiva"* (1907). Perhaps this can be applied to religious belief. The incredible religious myth or doctrine may allude in a veiled way to the reality of experiences that reason denies.

Where are these experiences lodged? We have to find an area of psychic experience, no longer accessible to consciousness, in which the continuance of belief is essential for happiness, and even for survival. This suggests that faith has its earliest origins in the confidence of the young infant that the anxieties which threaten him will prove illusory, and that religion re-creates the myths (fantasies, illusions, perhaps delusions) by means of which the child held on to or justified his conviction. Religion, Winnicott (1971) said, is one of the transitional phenomena in the potential space between mother and infant. Perhaps this accounts for the fact which puzzled Freud, that the first deities were the great mother goddesses. Religious belief proclaims the infant's knowledge that, come what may, "the everlasting arms" of the mother will be there.

What are the special characteristics of Christianity? And what are the particular demands that it makes upon faith? Finally, what is the significance of these questions for post-Christian man, who often appears to be more dependent on psychoanalysis than on religion?

First, I would like to state what I consider to be the distinguishing features of the Christian religion. It is impossible to do this uncontroversially at any level. Christianity derives from many sources—Jewish, Greek, Zoroastrian. Christ's teaching is portrayed in gospels of differing orientations and contains a number of apparent contradictions. The Christian religion was molded as a revolutionary force under the influence of Augustine's elaboration of the Pauline doctrine of predestination. This austere doctrine was reiterated by Luther and Calvin. It has been softened by the doctrine of free will enshrined eventually in Aquinas's summary. My own account of the salient features of Christianity is based on its development to the end of the nineteenth century, since which time, in my opinion, its intellectual influence has declined. My account therefore gives due weight to the Protestant doctrines which triumphed in the countries industrialized early. I recognize that some may consider that the importance of such features as the Christian ethic of love, demonstrated by good works, has been undervalued.

1. Christianity is a monotheistic religion in which man and God have become *identified*. In Christ, the *logos,* the principle of the universe, was made flesh. God became a perfect man, and a man could be God without shedding his human characteristics. Moreover, the godhead became a unified Trinity. If Ernest Jones (1923) is right that the three Persons of the Trinity unconsciously represent father, mother, and child, then the remarkable fact is that they are fused without strife or ambivalence. Historically and psychologically, Western man derived immense power from the new mutual involvement of God and man. In this, Christianity may be contrasted with the religions of the Semitic desert tribes (such as the Jews) who took as their God a tribal father, with Manicheism which made man an intermediary between the contending

forces of light and dark, and with the strict intellectual monotheism of later paganism. Christianity represents an immense new assertion of the spiritual power of man, to which Christian martyrs bore witness from the beginning.

2. The individual soul is stamped forever by the test of this life. It is not punished by being degraded to a lower form of existence or rewarded by being reborn in a higher state, nor are a man's sins visited on his descendants. In an increasingly strong current of Christian thought, the individual soul is once and for all either blessed or damned to eternity. This austere doctrine derives from the later Jewish belief in Gehenna, but Gehenna was a special part of Sheol, the abode of shades, just as Tartarus, which first appears in Roman writers at about the time of Virgil, was a special part of Hades, reserved for the torment of particular sinners. In popular Jewish teaching the nature of the afterlife has remained rather ill-defined, whereas for most of the Christian epoch the fate of the soul for eternity has been paramount in popular consciousness. The Christian belief here again asserts an heroic view of the vitality and power of the spirit of man, and the abysmal nature of any failure.

3. This soul of divine origin is at odds with the body. This doctrine "introduced into European culture a new interpretation of human existence, the interpretation we call puritanical" (Dodds 1965). It laid the basis for a constant sense of man's failure, as his divine soul struggled hopelessly against his flesh.

4. The doctrine of predestination, especially in its Augustinian formulation. Man's *cor irrequietum* (unquiet heart) struggled against the pleasures of evil, which were "inflicted on the memory" so that the pleasure of each act was amplified by being remembered and repeated. From such a state man could not hope to be saved unless God elected to call him. Tremen-

dous efforts would be necessary for any man to convince himself that he was numbered among the Elect. This was "a doctrine for hard times" (Brown 1967) as the Roman world broke up under barbarian invasion, civil wars, epidemics and galloping inflation. It was repeated by Luther and Calvin as the medieval world broke up under the impact of modern commerce and industry.

I should like at this point to summarize my argument, expand the main points and state their implications. Religious faith has its origins in the fantasies which the infant creates to justify its confidence that the mother will continue to protect and rule its world, and will be there—from the infant's point of view—forever. The degree of confidence in its ultimately being protected which the child develops gives it the courage to be adventurous. The experiences on which this confidence is based are no longer available to conscious memory; but affective conviction bears witness, as in some screen memories, to the operation of displacement of a sense of reality from unknown psychic events. In these circumstances the experiences can be affirmed or revived only by symbolic means. The symbols have to be taken as literal truths because this provides the only means of conveying the truth of the experiences. It is because religious faith indicates that a child has developed real confidence in its ability to survive psychic dangers that it is taken as a test of individual character. The irrational component of religion—the swearing that nonsense is truth—is a test of social cohesiveness of a comparable kind. The individual's ability to conform in asserting irrational beliefs is supposed to measure the degree to which he will abandon his selfish and opportunistic interests for the sake of society.

The acceptance of religion as a test of social reliability has grown increasingly severe in human history. The great mother religions of the East centerd on deities of the soil which reconciled man to the order of nature. As the Aryan tribes moved forward, somewhere about 2000 b.c., the gods became detached from the soil, and religions developed in which the moral imperative was not disengagement and reconciliation with nature, but involvement in fighting for right against wrong, and religions such as the Semitic religions or Zoroastrianism developed. Then finally, with the tasks imposed by the breakup of the Pax Romana, Western man adopted a religion which put on him a moral test of the utmost stringency. Whether he passed or failed it in one life, as has been said, would seal the fate of his soul forever—apart from a slight concession about Purgatory. With the breakup of the medieval order and its replacement by an increasingly complex commercial and industrial organization, these doctrines were asserted even more harshly. Purgatory was abolished. Every man was damned (save, following Augustine, a number limited to the number of fallen angels) unless called to Election by God's Grace, bestowed not for good works (which belonged to the world and therefore to the Devil who ruled it) but for faith in God's justice.

The development of a child's faith is sorely tested by such a religion, which may even lead to what George Steiner (1971) has called "the nostalgia for disaster." It is reasonable to suppose that a number of strong cohesive forces in the environment of the growing child will usually be required to maintain the growth of faith begun in early infancy.

Some years ago I had a patient whose analysis was the stimulus to these reflections by illustrating the dangers to which the development of faith could be exposed in childhood. Though not consciously religious, he could not escape the feeling that he was damned. This feeling had developed when he became unfaithful to his wife. She had represented "a childhood dream." She "had rescued him and made him what he was" and "everything that he had become he owed to her." The woman with whom he had started the love affair was a writer whom he considered a genius. What pleased him most about the book they wrote together, and gave him reassurance, was that no one could tell which parts were written by him and which by her; but he also felt that she stole his soul.

He could tell me quite early in his analysis what was the worst fate he knew, surely relevant for the ultimate horror of damnation. This was having to love two women. There could be no greater agony than needing both, since to have both was impossible. He could also tell me something about damnation itself: it was the third term in a series, the first two of which were inertia and madness.

The feeling that he was damned was not the only cause of his coming to me. The immediate cause was that he had stammered in a speech. This threatened his career outside literature as it depended on his oratory. But he also complained of a lack of "reciprocity" with his wife, with whom he was impotent, and was worried by a preoccupation with women in trousers or severely masculine clothes.

He recognized his preoccupation with damnation as a neurotic rumination but he also felt that it manifested itself by everything going wrong for him. As an example he gave his previous analysis. During the whole year that it lasted the analyst had said virtually nothing, and had then written him a letter one weekend telling him that he did not see any point in his coming back. A fantasy about the analyst, who had died some years before he came to me, brought damnation into the new transference more directly. He wanted me to report him to the Institute of Psycho-Analysis, and thus in effect bring about his punishment after death. This (as well as other factors) gave his fantasy about damnation a psychotic tinge.

I would like to leave his sexuality and even his splitting mechanisms on one side as far as possible (though they are relevant) and consider only that part of the patient's experience of illness which is most directly related to the propositions I have put forward about religious faith and traditional Christian theology.

His feeling of being damned had been formed when he had started to leave the one person who had "rescued him and made him what he was"—that is, when he betrayed his creator and savior. This was not the first time he had betrayed someone who filled these two roles, nor was it the last, since, in my view, he did so again in some measure in the transference. His mother had rescued him from the disruption caused by his father, an obsessional architect who disregarded all household routine. She had turned to the literary education of her only child and fostered the artistic values which were so important to him. When she left home however, he refused to accompany her, living instead with his father, whom he experienced (rather like the woman with whom he later collaborated) as "an ageless being from another world." However, his father eventually left too for the more timeless life of his club, and it was from the misery of solitude that his wife had rescued him.

The rescue was effective in so far as it gave my patient adequate conditions for his career, and eventually his two careers. He achieved some minor success in literature. However, he read a book which changed his life. He was converted to the aims it expressed, and he founded an organization to establish them. Though these were orientated towards the past, they had a liberating social purpose, giving new life to obsolescent means of communication, and incidentally providing him with most of his income. His powers of molding an audience and persuading backers were impressive, and he described himself as a Prometheus (though he also feared that he might sway millions to their detriment). He seemed transfigured after a speech—he had also had an experience of transfiguration as a child. His wife appeared in the eyes of the world to give him a considerable reciprocity by a happy, if subordinate and self-sacrificing, collaboration with him in his work. However, although he had enjoyed sexual intercourse with her before they were married, his sexual life with her "petered out" within a year as he became increasingly preoccupied with women in masculine clothes.

The emergence of his feelings of being damned seems to me to have followed a classic pattern. In Christian theology the worst torment of the damned is the knowledge that they have deprived themselves of the bliss of union with God, who (as Christ) died to save them, by their own repudiation of him. The first of the damned were the fallen angels, led by Lucifer, the Light-Bearer—just as the first to be utterly cast out was Adam, who ate of the fruit of the Tree of Knowledge, also called the Tree of Life, which made men as Gods. Lucifer's sin was considered by Origen to have been pride, and his view was supported by Athanasius in the East and Augustine in the West. Combining the stories of Lucifer and of Adam, it could be said that the liberator who bears the Light becomes proud of his knowledge to the extent that he utterly loses the paradise of reciprocal converse with his Creator. The next event recorded of Adam, following his acquisition of shame over his genitals, was that he was unable to talk with God when God walked in the Garden in the cool of the day. Many other Western myths support the interpretation that it is pride in knowledge that leads to damnation: for instance, Prometheus stole the fire of the Gods after learning to make men out of clay, while Faust was threatened with damnation as a result of his wish to proceed from his knowledge of the physical world to a unity of knowledge of things seen and unseen which would enable him to control it.

My patient's two women stood for his father and mother. His mother had inspired him through literature, but his father (while deploring such useless tastes) induced awe in him by his power of disruption of his mother's world combined with stories of the quite different life open to people of discrimination in his bachelor days before 1914. These two powerful figures quarrelled with each other incessantly. Faced with the unending struggle of each parent to possess his soul he could end only by removing himself from both of them physically, as far as he could, and from their psychological influence by denigrating them. He regressed to narcissism and became "a potentate" organizing imaginary countries in great detail, and he remained to some extent a potentate and savior in the organization he had founded. The hell that was mobilized in his love life by his conflict over his two women was the result of his inertia in finding a solution to the repetition of his childhood problem of how to serve and unite the parents whom he loved, and the madness and self-reproach to which his conflict over their irreconcilability had brought him. Damnation was the final term in a series which began with his paralysis in this task.

What has all this to do with the genesis of the cardinal sin of pride? The child of quarrelling parents is forced to judge them at a time when the ego is still functioning on an all-or-none basis in respect of love and hate. The still extant purified pleasure ego is inflated by the comparison which the developing critical faculties make between itself and its debased objects. On the other hand, since it still operates basically as a pleasure-ego, and not as a discriminating adult ego, it cannot make the careful value judgments which are achieved only by the integration of the impulse-life with reality testing. As a result, there are insufficient realistic images of the parents for healthy identification and fusion of the images. The ego is further weakened by the parents' competition for the child, played out as seduction. The end result of all this is that he enters the oedipal period with sexuality and aggression both powerfully stimulated, but without adequate realistic powers of assessment to control his omnipotent fantasies. This fateful combination of insufficiently bridled impulse and inadequate strength of inner objects exposes him both to "the sin of pride" and the inevitability of an immense sense of failure, since the pride is not linked with a realistic appraisal of the possibilities of achievement. When all the narcissism which has been induced by the parents' seduction is condensed with the sense of failure, and with the omnipotent and debased introjects, the result can be well summed up as damnation.

But my patient had also had an experience of salvation: his conversion to the cause he served after reading a book. Now his organization, if successful, would establish a sort of dream city and state in reality, quite apart from any function it might have in giving him an empire to administer as a potentate. If he had a religious faith, then it was his faith in the aims for which his organization strove, and in his role as savior.

The experiences which lay behind this faith were greatly clarified when certain memories were lifted from repression after three years. They were organized around his memory of regularly watching his mother urinate through a hole which was "both there and not there at the same time"—probably the hole in her combinations [the back flap in her long underwear—ed.]. His vision of beauty and mystery radiated from this experience, the flow of urine being condensed with the flow of milk from the breast as the source of spiritual and to some extent physical grace. The memory also of course contained important determinants of his fetishism.

The condensation of milk and urine, the intensity of his identification with his urinating mother (as when in childhood he experienced "transfiguration" near the sea), and the close connection of these experiences with the creative use of his imagination, justify considering them as stemming from the phase of transitional phenomena. The experiences which his memory screened must have been intensely valuable; his whole system of ideals was orientated towards communication, reciprocity, and joy in culture and recreation. When he became able to reestablish his capacity for sexual intercourse (with a new girlfriend) he told me he felt like the man in a story who found a door in a wall which, once discovered, was ever longed for. It led to a garden where even the wild animals were tame. Surely this story referred to the taming of oral aggression by transitional experiences of play and reciprocity?

In later childhood, however, his joy in life turned sour. He had a screen memory of his mother reading *Treasure Island* to him, and of his father suddenly arriving at about ten o'clock at night and sweeping them off on holiday. This was an early version of being cast out. At school he had no real friends, only adherents. He had no interest in games; even when playing trains at home "the central experience was missing."

What prevented the further development of his capacity for "reciprocity" seems to be suggested by the screen memory I have described. Quarrels and disunity among the parents so weaken the image of each of them and so stimulate the child's attack that he has only damaged or revengeful images for introjection. As a result there is, so to speak, no unified family Trinity left to give the strength of mature identification necessary to transform the early identification with the mother into an identification based on sympathy and reciprocity. Though this patient's symptom was articulated with particular clarity, I think that we see a number of patients who feel damned, and I have always thought that a fundamental disunity between the parents (though it is sometimes masked) is an important etiological factor.

I have emphasized the importance of a lack of cohesion between the parents for the genesis of the feeling of being damned in the individual. Although there is a danger of facile generalization in extrapolating from individual to social psychology, it may be significant that there was a marked lack of cohesion in society at the time that the doctrine of damnation was emphasized so forcefully by Augustine and when it was reemphasized by Luther and Calvin during the Reformation. In the third and fourth centuries the *Pax Romana* died under the impact of barbarian invasion and vast social change. "You could pile one religious insurance on another and still not feel safe" (Dodds 1965). According to Augustine, every man would be damned unless specially called by God as a father calls his son. This sense of election could then unite the urbanized poor, the ruined peasant or *rentier*, the manumitted slave, the demobilized soldier and the intellectual into one classless society, "members one of another." Thus, the doctrine of damnation could provide a sound social and moral doctrine for confused people and be incorporated into a religion suitable to dominate the Empire.

The same was true as the medieval world broke up under the impact of expanding commerce and industry. Though the doctrine of predestination to damnation was invoked by Luther to separate man from the modern world and not to facilitate his transition to it, it was used to give the rising middle classes of the sixteenth and seventeenth (and nineteenth) centuries confidence in their salvation and victory.

The popularity of the doctrine of damnation played a similar role in society and in my patient: if evil was inflicted on the soul by Original Sin, it was outside the area of human choice, and its presence did not immediately imply the soul's corruption. With my patient, the more the supernatural asserted its claims (as it also did in his writings), and the more he felt damned, the more he felt his rational soul to be free and at a distance from his persecuting inner objects.

I have suggested that the need to split good and evil in the soul was related to the increasing complexity of the tasks of society, just as in my patient it related to the impossibility of making a choice between the conflicting demands of his parents. It seems to me that increasing complexities of civilization demand ever more discrimination of judgment. This discrimination of judgment is transmitted by the parents early in the child's life. The world of social relationships becomes increasingly complex and subtle. This encourages the early dethronement of the parents—that is, the early tasting of the fruit of the Tree of Knowledge, which Western man has always been convinced leads straight to disaster. The disaster in a complex modern culture is the failure to maintain the early faith that leads to object constancy.

REFERENCES

Arlow, J. A. (1961). Ego psychology and the study of mythology. *Journal of the American Psychoanalytic Association* 9:371-393.
Brown, P. (1967). *Augustine of Hippo.* London: Faber.
Dodds, E. R. (1965). *Pagan and Christian in an Age of Anxiety.* Cambridge University Press.
Freud, S. (1900). The interpretation of dreams. *Standard Edition* 4 and 5.
——— (1907). Delusions and dreams in Jensen's *Gradiva. Standard Edition* 9:7-95.
——— (1913). Totem and taboo. *Standard Edition* 13:1-161.
——— (1918). From the history of an infantile neurosis. *Standard Edition* 17:7-122.

———— (1927). The future of an illusion. *Standard Edition*. 21:3-56.

———— (1930). Civilization and its discontents. *Standard Edition*. 21:59-145.

———— (1939). Moses and monotheism. *Standard Edition* 23:7-937.

Fromm, E. (1963). *The Dogma of Christ: Religion, Psychology and Culture.* London: Routledge and Kegan Paul.

Jones, E. (1923). A psycho-analytic study of the Holy Ghost concept. In *Essays in Applied Psycho-Analysis.* London: Hogarth Press.

Reik, T. (1958). *Myth and Guilt: The Crime and Punishment of Mankind.* London: Hutchinson.

Steiner, G. (1971). *In Bluebeard's Castle: Notes towards the Redefinition of Culture.* London: Faber.

Tolstoy, L. (1903). *Resurrection.* London: Grant Richards.

Winnicott, D. W. (1971). *Playing and Reality.* London: Tavistock.

Index

Fear (*continued*)
  by primitive defenses,
    19–20
  See also anxiety
Feces, as cash to analyst, 102–103
Fenichel, O., 93, 162
Ferenczi, S., 4
Flew, A., 186
Fliess, W., 115
Flying phobia, 67
French, T. M., 5
Freud, A., 46, 84, 111, 124, 134
Freud, S., xii, xiii, xv, xvi, xxiii,
    xxx, 4, 5, 15, 16, 22, 26,
    27, 30, 32, 39, 41, 46, 54,
    56, 68, 77, 78, 88, 110, 112,
    115, 124, 126, 128, 157,
    161, 163, 165, 169, 171,
    172, 175–76, 178, 182, 184,
    185, 191, 193, 194, 195,
    199, 201, 206, 207, 208
  and analyst's identity, 175–76
Fromm, E., 5, 206

Gardiner, P., 192, 199
Genetic approach and historical
    method, 185
Genetic fallacy, H. Hartmann's,
    26–27
George III, 199
Gillespie, 14
Gitelson, M., 49, 127, 135
Glover, E., 133
Gombrich, E., 114, 115
Greenson, P., 47

Hartmann, H., 26, 47, 92, 185
  genetic fallacy of, 26–27
Heimann, P., 6, 30, 47, 127, 135

Hell, concept of, 210, 216
  See also damnation
Helmholtz, 27
Heraclitus, 197n
Herodotus, 188
Historical method in
    psychoanalysis, xvii–xviii,
    xxv, 181, 185–87, 188–90,
    192–202
  as artificial distinction, 188–90
  and genetic approach, 185
  and identification, 196
  and philosophy, 186–87
  and prediction, 200
  and psychoanalytic
    controversies, 202–202
  and repetition and
    reconstruction, 197–98
  and transference, 196–97, 199
Hoffer, W., 6, 47
Home, H. J., 187
Hyman, S. E., 170

Id derivatives, dreams indicating
    ego's attempt to integrate,
    22–23
Idealized object, patient's
    dependency on, 97–98
Identification
  and historical method, 196
  mutual
    and object relationship,
      48–50
    steps for maintenance of,
      50–51
  spontaneity in, 115–16
Identity
  of analyst, 161–80